THE VOGUE SEWING BOOK OF FITTING, ADJUSTMENTS, AND ALTERATIONS

PUBLISHED BY
BUTTERICK FASHION
MARKETING COMPANY
NEW YORK, N. Y.

Library of Congress Catalog Card Number 72-83049

First Edition

Copyright © 1972 by
Butterick Fashion Marketing Company
A Division of American Can Company
161 Sixth Avenue
New York, New York 10013

Printed in the U.S.A.
by the Butterick Plant, Altoona, Pa.

THE VOGUE SEWING BOOK OF FITTING, ADJUSTMENTS, AND ALTERATIONS

EDITOR
Patricia Perry

TECHNICAL COORDINATOR
Elizabeth Musheno

COPY EDITOR
Alice Rohrbacher

WRITERS
Marion Bartholomew, Paige Camp,
Connie Meyer, Carol Sherman

ART EDITOR
Tony Serino

ARTISTS
Susan Frye, Janet Lombardo,
Barbara Hanlon, Karen Coughlin,
Marilyn Gong

PRODUCTION COORDINATORS
Paul Milbauer, Lou Borsato,
Susanne Olson, Doreen Williams

FASHION COORDINATOR
Susan Leve

MARKETING DIRECTOR
John Skeels

SALES MANAGER
Don Schmidt

PRODUCT MANAGER
Pam Guyot

Preface

Of the many talented women who sew, there are those who are quite capable of selecting the latest fashion silhouette to flatter their figures and then choosing the perfect fabric to complement it. Their buttonholes are flawless and their hems are perfectly turned, but somehow the total fashion picture seems to lack a most important quality—FIT!

Creating a garment which fits perfectly is no accident. It is a result of time, patience, an understanding of the problem, and an insight into resolving it. Remember, because a woman's figure is constantly changing, her fitting experience or education must be comprehensive enough to accommodate all the different fitting situations she is going to encounter.

In this book, no attempt has been made to distinguish between the serious sewer, who looks upon each of her efforts as a further development of her art, and the casual sewer whose main purpose is simply to create as many new clothes for herself as she can. Both sewers can benefit from the information they will find between these covers.

For the former, this book will attempt to unravel some of the heretofore *mysteries* of fitting. In plain language it will document and answer problems in theory as well as in fact. It will undertake to describe in detail the subtleties of fit, to distinguish good fit from bad, and to avoid the most glaring error of the amateur—over-fitting! For the latter, the prospect of perfect fit should entice her into learning more about this interesting art. Every effort has been made to prove that, even though a garment is of little monetary significance, there is no reason for it to suffer from poor fit or second-rate workmanship.

It is hoped that even the most expert sewer will find this book to be a new adventure in sewing. She will find that some fitting methods are as familiar as old friends, while others stimulate her to think about new ways of solving familiar problems. In either case, from what she will learn, she will be able to approach her art with the confidence of the professional.

Patricia Perry

Contents

BOOK I

The Art of Creative Fashion Fitting

Fashion Prelude
A Fitting Beginning

We live in an era of jumbo jets and instant communication and still there are things that by their very nature take time. Few women can manage to look attractive without working at it a bit. Those women who look fabulous are those women who have accepted a fact of life—hard work is behind the art of beauty. For the seamstress who wants her garment to fit well and flatter her, this will not come instantly. The creative dressmaker, whether a beginner or an experienced hand, must acknowledge that the art of fitting is at the heart of effective fashion, and it requires patience.

We have all had the disappointing experience of constructing a garment that did not fit. An ill-fitting garment can make even a good figure look bad. Imagine what poor fit does to the woman who needs more than the average amount of fitting changes! It is not professional to choose the finest fabrics, use your best skills, and then produce a garment that looks homemade because it does not fit. With this book, Vogue Patterns will help you attain the fitting skills that will add another dimension to your home sewing, and permit you to shine as an individual in a professionally fitted garment.

Let's be perfectly honest at the outset. Many women are really reluctant to take the time to fit properly, or to fit at all. Perhaps the woman who sews is fearful because she does not know how to fit, and that keeps her from attempting it. Certainly she is neither lazy nor unimaginative, or she would not be sewing!

We at Vogue Patterns feel that when the mystery and mystique of fitting are put aside, that tiny bit of apprehension will disappear. Once you gain the "eye" and the control, and understand the principles of fitting, solving the old problems will seem simple, and each new problem can be looked upon as a challenge.

Yourself . . . And Environs

The standards of good fit are influenced by many things. The current fashion silhouette and design, the characteristic hang or drape of your fabric, the amount of ease, and your posture and figure type are all interrelated elements in producing a well-fitting garment. This will make you look good and feel comfortable while moving, standing, or sitting. It hangs on the body without wrinkling, pulling, or sagging. A garment can be over-fitted, causing loss of comfort as well as loss of style line. A garment that is under-fitted just misses its chance to be chic and figure-flattering.

Your adult height and bone structure are relatively constant, but your weight and shape may shift, depending on your age, diet, body chemistry . . . and your undergarments. Before beginning to fit, we might consider changing two important things that will affect fitting problems. If you are ten or twenty pounds overweight, it is probably within your control to do something about it. Even a loss of five pounds would help in reducing your bulk and the accompanying problems of fit. If your posture is not good, you can try to improve it with the proper exercising. Most well-dressed women "walk tall." Being aware that you can stand straighter and taller anytime you wish is good medicine. A small weight loss and any improvement in your posture might lead to a noticeable change in the way you look even before you consider fit. Let's take the time now to see how your posture "stands up" to scrutiny.

Posture

The ever-so-erect clothes-horse as a standard of beauty has all but disappeared. Today's fashionable woman strives for a natural look. She wishes to be judged by her accomplishments as a human being, whether wife, mother, teacher, doctor, lawyer, or business woman. The pride and poise that come with accomplishment will do much to aid posture, since good posture is an expression of good physical and mental health. Medical doctors, psychiatrists, and physical fitness experts all agree that posture communicates your attitude about yourself and the world. In terms of body language, the woman who stands up tall has taken a positive stand in the world.

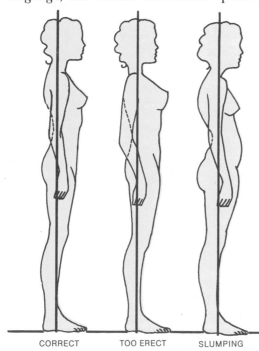

CORRECT   TOO ERECT   SLUMPING

Good posture is natural in that it is comfortable and healthful for the body. The rigid or extremely erect figure produces tension and strain, especially in the knees and back muscles. It shortens the distance from back of neck to shoulder blades, and lengthens the distance from base of neck to apex of bust thereby causing fitting problems. The opposite of this rigid posture is the slump, which is all too familiar. Slumping with the chin thrust forward, the chest sunken, and the stomach protruding will produce rounded shoulders, fatigue, and backache. Dowager's hump, sway back, and protruding abdomen are fitting problems which may evolve from slumping.

Naturally, you are wondering how your posture compares to the illustration of good posture. To test this, stand with your back against a wall and your weight resting on your feet. If posture is correct, your shoulders, shoulder blades, and buttocks should touch the wall; you should barely be able to insert your hand between the wall and the small of the back. If only your shoulders touch the wall, your posture is too erect. If only your shoulder blades touch, you are round-shouldered. A woman with large buttocks might appear to have bad posture when in fact she does not; her derrière touches the wall sooner than her shoulders and shoulder blades. For reasons like this, use judgment with this guide.

Do not be disheartened if the preceding test pointed out the fact that you have bad posture, for it can be corrected and improved by the following exercises. Walking is excellent for improving posture. Get into the habit of walking instead of hopping into the car or onto a bus for those fifteen-minute trips! When sitting and doing hand work, sit as tall as possible with your feet flat on the floor and your weight evenly distributed. Do not twist or wrap your leg around the chair leg. Because your lower back should be supported by the chair, a chair with a hard back is best. When at the sewing machine, lean forward from the hip. Good posture at the machine increases efficiency by giving you more visibility and more leverage for manual dexterity, and reduces strain on neck and shoulders. Get up and stretch now and then to ease strain and fatigue. When standing and fitting at your dress form, stretch your body upward against the pull of gravity.

But do not get carried away! Trying to do posture exercises at the sewing machine or when you are fitting may make you unable to concentrate on the job at hand. In the long run, *thinking* posture is almost certain to improve posture to some extent.

The pull of gravity causes additional posture and health problems to the woman who is overweight. Being overweight causes redistribution of the weight so that it does not fall in a plumb line over the knee cap and the arch of the foot. This can cause foot problems as well as backache. Excess weight also strains the muscles so that they cannot hold the chest, stomach, and buttocks in their proper positions; these areas then sag. The strain on the entire frame can cause a reduction in height, since the excess weight is pulling down and straining the muscles which are unable to hold the body erect against the pull of gravity. This downward pull on the body reduces height and inevitably leads to slumping. The compact figure without excess weight can maintain the muscular tension necessary to hold the organs and their surrounding flesh in place without strain, and can thus stand at full height comfortably. The overweight woman must work harder to stand up straight and often succeeds less because of her bulk.

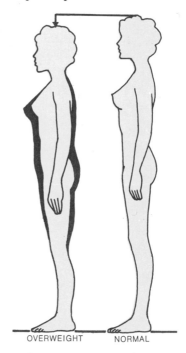

OVERWEIGHT   NORMAL

Undergarments will help support her weight, but will not eliminate the problem.

What if, after all your efforts to lose a few pounds, to pull in that stomach, and tuck in that derrière, nothing happens, and you are still facing that sagging you in the fitting mirror? Since it is easier to fit a figure that you like, rather than one that you dislike, try this last resort to eliminate that sagginess. Those wonderful people who invented undergarments must have known that the spirit may be willing, but the flesh is certainly weak. Purchase well-fitted undergarments for a controlled or more youthful figure. You are not the first to do so and will not be the last!

Undergarments

The flora and fauna of the undergarment world are so abundant that one would be hard put to keep track of all the newest ones. In the age of the no-bra bra and the ungirdled girth, there are still dozens of bra styles, endless girdle variations, and all-in-one foundation garments. With all these to evaluate, how can you decide which undergarments are meant for you? The decision is directly related to the function and fit of the undergarments with your figure and the clothes you'll be wearing.

A *youthful, firm* figure needs only a soft bra and panties of nylon or tricot. For a figure that *needs a little support* due to sagging busts or abdomen, or hip or thigh bulge, choose a bra to fit and support the breasts, and a girdle to firm up the problem area. If a panty girdle is preferred, make sure the crotch and buttocks shaping will be comfortable and not flatten the derrière, especially in pants. A *mature, heavier* figure looks best in an all-in-one foundation which eliminates midriff bulge.

The person who can help you the most in the selection of correctly fitting undergarments is the fitter or corsetière in your specialty shop or department store. Do not be satisfied until you have arrived at your most comfortable and sleek look, even though it may take endless trying on and patience. Do not select undergarments when you are in a hurry or when you intend to lose a few pounds.

To choose the correct bra size, measure snugly around the rib cage just under the bust, and add 5″ to that measurement; for figures measuring more than 38″, add 3″. For cup size, measure above the breasts, then subtract that figure from the bra size. If the difference is 1″, wear an A-cup; 2″, B; 3″, C; 4″, D. If your rib cage is disproportionately smaller than your bust development, there will be variations from the above formula when measuring cup size. Complete instructions for taking your body measurements are on pages 22–23, but be aware that determining your bra size is different from measuring your bust.

When you have chosen undergarments which will minimize your figure flaws, make sure they do not create other problems for you when fitting—excessively tight bras or girdles cause rolls of fat to ripple unbecomingly above or below them. Two bras may seem alike to you but they may not be: one may have a soft, smooth apex, while the other may have more lift and a pronounced shape. During every fitting, *you must wear the same undergarments* that will be worn with the completed garment to avoid repeated changes in the placement of bust darts, over-the-bust seaming, waistline seams or darts, and darts at hip.

Surroundings

Now that you have decided to take a good long look at your figure and the fit of your clothes, you will need the proper environment in which to really see them. Just as you have arranged to have a small corner of your own where you can sew in an organized and peaceful way, so should your fitting environment be arranged. It is best if your cutting and sewing area are close together. The number of things that contribute to a good fitting environment is not great, but each is an important aid.

☐ The space you choose for fitting should be well lighted, with both overhead and natural light. Be wary of spotlighting, as it tends to produce shadows. A high-intensity lamp is handy for checking details.

☐ Have a full-length mirror that is placed in such a way that you are not "cut off" at the ankles or at the top of your hair-do. A three-way mirror is ideal, since it enables you to get a full back and side view.

☐ The space should be decorated in a soft color that will not clash with any garment you will be fitting. Avoid hanging bright, large prints behind you that would fight with the look and line of your fashion.

☐ Be sure there is room for you to step back, turn, and pivot. Do not stand toe-to-toe with your mirror. There should be enough room for you to walk toward the mirror to see what happens when you move in your garment. You might want to place a chair in front of the mirror to observe your skirt hemline when seated.

☐ A table on which to place some of your fitting equipment should be close at hand. One that is elbow height is most convenient. A shaving stand or a planter is often just the right height and size to hold your tape measure, chalk, and pins.

☐ There should be closet space for garments in progress, as it is encouraging and professional to see an emerging dress—no matter how incomplete—hanging there. This will also save time by precluding unnecessary pressing. Protection from dust and soil is another benefit—especially if you are one to put projects aside for awhile. Place your garment on wooden or padded hangers, unless you are working in a stretchy fabric.

☐ Look at your garment from different angles; when you walk into your sewing room, glance at it from the doorway. What is your honest reaction? Do not love your garment so much that you cannot see its faults on and off your body.

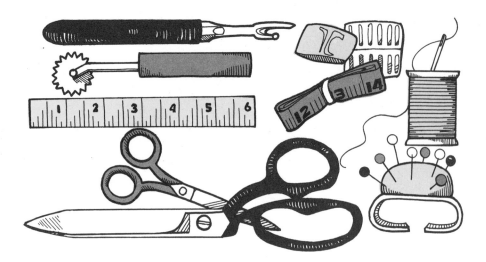

TOOLS AND EQUIPMENT: Much of the equipment you are accustomed to using for sewing is also used for fitting and for flat pattern adjustments and alterations. Listed below are the hand tools necessary for those procedures.

Rulers are essential. Use a 6″ ruler with an indicator for small changes. An 18″ see-through ruler is invaluable for flat pattern work as it has lengthwise and crosswise ⅛″ markings.

T-Squares are shaped like a T and used to determine cross grains and to alter patterns. A 9″ plastic T-square with a 4″ T-span is adequate for pattern work. An L-square can also be used.

French Curves are used to draw curved lines for necklines, armholes, and seams. The patternmaker's French curve is made of see-through plastic and is shaped like a large J. Its graduated curves are used in a manner similar to a ruler but on curved pattern areas.

Yardsticks should be smoothly finished. They are used to check grainlines, mark hems while fitting, and to blend seamlines when making pattern changes.

Tissue Paper is essential for pattern adjustments. It is used for lengthening and filling in adjusted garment areas on the pattern pieces. Use white, wrinkle-free tissue paper.

Pattern Weights are used in flat pattern work to keep the pattern in position while you transfer any changes or make adjustments. If these are not available to you, use book ends or some other heavy, compact household object.

Tape is used to make pattern changes permanent. Choose any type that will take markings as new cutting lines or construction lines may need to be re-drawn over the tape.

Marking Pens are excellent for making final notations on pattern pieces. Do not use ball point pens that are smudgy. Since marking is subject to change during fitting, do not get trigger-happy with felt tip pens.

Iron-on Non-woven Interfacing or Transparent Non-woven Nylon Fabric can be used to make your master pattern a valuable sewing tool. On pages 183-185 you will find instructions telling you how to use these products.

Dressmaker's Silk Pins are recommended for fitting. However, colored plastic-head pins will emphasize an area that needs changes. Avoid holding pins in your mouth, as smudges of lipstick can suddenly appear on your garment.

Pin Cushions of the wrist type are best for fitting.

Muslin is unbleached and comes in light to heavy weights. Light- or medium weight muslin is best for constructing and testing for a fitting, depending on the garment style. Medium weight is most often used. Heavyweight muslin can be used if you are trying out a coat or jacket pattern.

Tape Measures that are most accurate are made of non-stretch wire and plastic, and are printed on both sides. To measure a curve, place edge of tape along seamline, moving it slowly for accuracy.

Dressmaking Shears with 7"–9" blades and a bent handle are best. Never use your shears to cut anything but fabric. Shears that are dropped or nicked will damage fabric during cutting.

Trimming Scissors with 5"–6" long blades are used for clipping areas that need to be released while fitting.

Needles and Thread will be used for thread tracing and basting. Match needle size to thread and fabric. Cotton or silk thread is suitable. However, when using contrasting colors, keep them light. Excessive dye or thread tufts may leave permanent marks on light or white fabrics.

Dressmaker's Tracing Paper is used to transfer markings from pattern to fabric or muslin by tracing markings with the tracing wheel. Mark carefully and slowly, and be wary of a color that is not removable when working in fabric. When marking two layers of fabric, the double-faced tracing paper is a time-saver.

Tracing Wheels come with a plain edge, a serrated edge, or a needlepoint edge. For transferring markings from pattern pieces to lightweight fabric or muslin, the plain or serrated edge is most effective. The needlepoint edge should be used on muslin or heavyweight fabric only. Be sparing in your use of the tracing wheel to avoid unnecessary distortion, even on patterns and muslin.

Tailor's Chalk or Dressmaker's Marking Pencils are used for marking any needed fitting changes. Test the chalk on your fabric before marking, since the wax type can be difficult to remove from hard-faced fabrics. Test it with your iron as well. Test the pencils the same way. A soft lead pencil with #2 lead will often do as well. In any marking, make sure that the method will not permanently damage or discolor the fabric, particularly if it is light-colored. It may be necessary to move darts and seamlines, so mark lightly but visibly.

Dress Forms can be found in many types; one that you can pin into is desirable when shaping areas like collars. It should have a heavy metal base.

Seam Rippers are great for releasing basting during a fitting.

Twill Tape is used to support fabric and to define lines.

Clothes Brushes are used to remove threads and lint so they will not distract from your fitting progress.

Cleaning Fluid might be needed. It is best to remove spots or stains before they set and before too many layers of construction make it more difficult to get at them. Refer to pages 51–53 in The Vogue Sewing Book for specific directions for spot and stain removal. Talcum powder is very effective in removing spots made by machine oil.

Skirt Markers are used for determining skirt lengths. There is a chalk type, a pin type, and a type which is a combination of both. The chalk type tends to leave marks. The pin type is best used with the help of another person.

USING A PLUMB LINE: A measuring device made by suspending a weight at one end of a cord is called a plumb line. It is used to determine true vertical direction. Construction engineers and carpenters work with a plumb line to help determine true perpendiculars and lines of stress. In very much the same way, the seamstress must work within the physical limitations of her media—fabric—with an awareness of its physical characteristics, i.e. its true perpendiculars and lines of stress.

An understanding of the use of a plumb line is related to an understanding of one of the most important physical characteristics of fabric—grain. (To make a plumb line, see The Vogue Sewing Book, page 132.) All fabrics have grain. In a garment cut on a true grain, the grain falls in straight, symmetrical lines. A lengthwise thread or seam runs perpendicular from the neck to the hem. A garment not cut on the true, straight grain will twist and sag across the center, or at one or both sides of the garment, distorting the straight grain. Grain is discussed at greater length on page 55.

When using the plumb line, it will be a great help for you if you have clearly indicated the straight grain by thread tracing the center of the sleeve, and the center front and center back of the garment (if there are no seams) along the lengthwise and crosswise threads of the fabric. When you are ready to check the grain at the center front and center back of your garment, tie the seam binding around your neck like a necklace and attach the plumb line. Place the line at the top of center thread tracing or the seam at both the front and back of the garment. To check side seams, tie the plumb line to a board and tuck it under your arm at the top of the seam. To check sleeve grains, have someone hold the plumb line at the shoulder seam and suspend it next to the sleeve; the grain will fall straight only to the elbow, so do not be concerned about the grain below this point.

The vertical seams and thread tracings should hang parallel to the plumb line, and the crosswise grain and thread tracings should be at right angles to it (exactly 90°). If they are not, mark the corrections with pins or chalk.

Once you have studied your fitting muslin or garment and determined the hang of the grain, enumerate the areas where the fabric grain is off-center or distorted, or mark them on your pattern illustration. Bone structure and posture as well as body contours will affect the hang of the grain; Book II on Adjustments and Book III on Alterations detail the causes and corrections required. Analyze as best you can what is causing the grain distortion for all problem areas. For minor adjustments, it is sometimes possible to open a faulty seam; smooth the fabric into position so that vertical and horizontal grains are at right angles (see page 56). Remember the golden rule of fitting—a law of physics, actually—for every **action** there is a **reaction**. For every tiny change, another part (or parts) of the garment will be affected. Accuracy in fitting depends on your ability to perceive this chain reaction.

THE DRESS FORM: It would be ideal to have someone who duplicated your figure perfectly. Then you could fit to your heart's content with confidence that the final garment would fit perfectly. But, fantasies aside, an exact duplicate of your body can never show the livability you need when in action. The dress form is the closest thing to a duplication of your figure. You will find that having one is a great aid in both fitting and construction.

Dress forms comes in a variety of types, and much depends on your figure and preferences when you are considering the purchase of one. Both the wire mesh type and the sectional type are limited in use, since they are not padded and smooth. The Unique dress form is of foam and is covered with a fabric shell which can be fitted to your individual figure. The professional dressmaker dummy is firm with fabric-covered cotton batting and usually has collapsable shoulders; it swivels in position, and the height is adjustable by means of a foot pedal. Most dress forms have a heavy metal base so that they will not tip over easily.

A dress form is invaluable because it enables you to check the general fit of the bodice, skirt, and sleeve, and to see if the hang of the grain is straight, and if darts, seams, neckline, and waistline are in place.

You can judge whether the roll of a collar and the lines of a lapel are smooth and symmetrical. Checking style details, like button placement and size, trims, and belts, is simpler with the dress form.

You can test the effects of color, texture, and proportions by combining fabrics on the dress form; merely place, rather than cut them.

Spot-steaming can be done on the dress form with a spray steam iron when you know your fabric, iron, and technique thoroughly. Follow your regular pressing techniques throughout construction.

MAKING A DRESS FORM COVER: The Unique foam dress form with adjustable cover enables you to get an exact replica of your figure. Follow the tips below:

The Unique foam form should be chosen by hip size and cover, if purchased, by bust size. When making your own cover, select a princess-style pattern with a jewel neckline. Choose the pattern by bust size; if you are between sizes, select the smaller size since the cover must be skin-tight. Cut off the pattern at mid-thigh length.

Buy two yards of heavy muslin, duck, denim, or canvas. Before cutting fabric, straighten its grain, pre-shrink, and press smooth.

Adjust the pattern to your length and circumference measurements. If working without a fitter, make a center front "Place on fold" line into a seam by adding a seam allowance. Allow for any asymmetrical figure faults.

Cut muslin from adjusted pattern, leaving 1½″ seam allowance on vertical seams. Mark seamlines and grainlines. Machine baste along marked seamlines.

Wear the undergarments and shoes you prefer—they affect weight distribution; do not wear a slip. Have your fitter pin the back seam for a skin-tight fit. Pin muslin to center front and center back of undergarments, securing neck, hip, and waist.

Follow the fitting points (pages 44–45), check shoulder seam, neck, underarm and armhole, seaming over bust contour, center front and center back seams, and side seams.

You can add a horizontal shaping seam across bust from center front seam to apex and from apex to side seam (similar to bra shaping); horizontal waistline shaping may be needed.

Mark the neckline, seams, shoulder line, and armholes. The armhole must fit high and tight. Add an armhole dart if you are very hollow at the armhole socket. When satisfied with the fit, mark changes and stitch cover permanently. Trim seams to ⅝″ and clip and notch to make seams duplicate body contours. Insert a separating zipper at center back seam. Try on muslin again; refine if needed. Encase neck and armholes with double-fold bias binding or fold-over braid.

You may want to mark your waistline, center front, and center back not indicated by a seam with ¼″ twill tape or ⅛″ soutache braid. Mark your bust apex in the same manner if you have not built in the bra shaping as suggested. Also mark the shapes and depths of your favorite necklines. To finish the lower edges, make a ½″ wide casing and insert twill tape, allowing for tie ends. Additional guidelines can be marked in chalk or magic marker.

Patterns . . . And You

The pattern industry today offers the creative dressmaker a potpourri of exciting fashion patterns that are technically perfect and that have built in fit to flatter any figure or size. It is in the evaluation of figure types and the selection of the pattern size that the seamstress determines the extent of personalized fitting she must do.

Size

Choosing the pattern size and correct figure type is probably the single most important decision made in arriving at good fit. Do not select your pattern size on the basis of the size that you take in ready-to-wear clothes. Instead, compare your measurements with the pattern specifications to make your decision. If your set of measurements (bust, waist, hips, and back length) do not exactly match those on the pattern measurement chart, you must decide which is most similar.

When selecting a dress, jacket, blouse, or coat pattern, choose your size by **bust** measurement. Body structure, weight, and pattern ease also influence the size you choose. If you are small-boned and between sizes, choose the smaller size; if you are large-boned and between sizes, choose the larger size. For a skirt, shorts, or pants pattern, select your size by waist measurement; if your hips are much larger or smaller than your waist, select the size closest to your hip measurement.

FIGURE TYPES: Height and proportions will also help you decide which figure type you are. Following is a list of Vogue Patterns' figure types. More details can be found in The Vogue Sewing Book (pages 108–111), in the back of the Vogue Patterns catalogue or in Vogue Pattern Book International.

Misses: A well-proportioned and developed figure that is 5'5"–5'6" without shoes.

Miss Petite: A well-proportioned, developed figure that is 5'2"–5'3" without shoes.

Women's: A larger, longer, and more fully developed figure than Misses; well-proportioned; 5'5"–5'6" without shoes.

Half-Size: A fully developed figure with short back waist; 5'2"–5'3" without shoes.

The pattern size and figure type does not guarantee good fit if you are not of statistically average measurements, or have figure or posture flaws. However, it is a starting point from which to begin custom fitting.

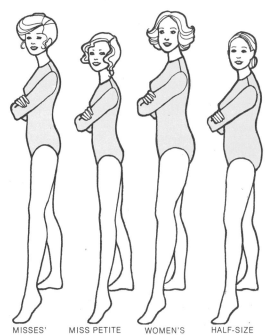

MISSES'   MISS PETITE   WOMEN'S   HALF-SIZE

MEASURING YOUR BODY: Precision work can hardly be considered an accident. Your measurements must be as precise as you can gauge them for they will be the foundation upon which your fashion garment will grow.

To begin with, choose the undergarments and shoes that will support and distribute your weight in a manner that pleases you. Work in front of the mirror when you are taking your measurements and make sure that the tape is held taut (not tight) against the body. The tape should lie flat and parallel to the floor when measuring most circumferences; do not let the tape slide down in front or back. Check the side view in the mirror to see that the tape is straight. The figures on page 23 will explain how to take your body measurements correctly.

Since these measurements will be referred to many times in the selection of your pattern size and later when you are doing adjustments and alterations, they should be kept in chart form for easy access. You should also make note of the date that the measurements are taken, as well as any future changes that may occur in your body shape. Body weight may not change, but your contours might; be aware that you could shift into a different size range and even figure type in time. It is recommended that you take your measurements periodically, so that your fashion sewing can consistently reflect the perfect fit for which you are striving.

Bust: Measure bust at fullest point with tape straight across back (1).

Chest: Measure at underarm above breasts (2).

Diaphragm: Measure around rib cage, halfway between bust and waist (3).

Waist: Tie string around torso at thinnest part; measure (4). (Keep string at waist until all measurements are taken.)

Hip: Mark tape position with pins on garment and measure from waist to pins to establish these hip positions when measuring. Record measurements. *High Hip:* Measure 2″–4″ below waist over top of hip bones (5). *Full Hip:* Measure at fullest part, usually 7″–9″ from waist (6). *Thigh Bulge:* With feet together, measure around both legs at fullest point of upper thigh (7).

Circumference of Leg: Measure leg at fullest part of thigh (8), knee (9), calf (10), and instep (11).

Neck: Measure circumference at the fullest part (12).

Front Neck to Waist: Measure from base of neck (the hollow between collar bones) to waist at center front (13).

Bust Point: Measure from prominent back neck bone over shoulder to bust point, and from bust point to center front at waist. Record measurements (14).

Shoulder: Measure along shoulder from base of neck to shoulder bone (15).

Arm Length: With arm slightly bent, measure from shoulder bone to elbow, and then to wrist above the little finger. Record both measurements (16).

Bicep: Measure at fullest part of upper arm, usually 1″ below armpit (17).

Cap Height: Measure from the bicep to the shoulder bone (18).

Wrist: Measure at wrist bone (19).

Back Neck to Waist: Measure from prominent neck bone at center back to waist (20).

Back Width: Measure from prominent neck bone down center back 4″–6″. At this point, measure across the back, with arms moderately forward, from the crease where arm meets body to the opposite crease (21).

Crotch Length: Sit on a hard, straight-backed chair; using a ruler, measure at side from waist to chair seat (22).

Pants Length: Measure at side from waist to floor, or to desired length (23).

Skirt Length: Measure from center back waist to desired hemline (24).

Dress, Jacket, Vest, or Blouse Length: Measure from prominent neck bone to desired position on torso for hem. Record these measurements for reference (not shown).

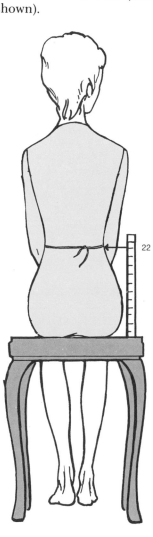

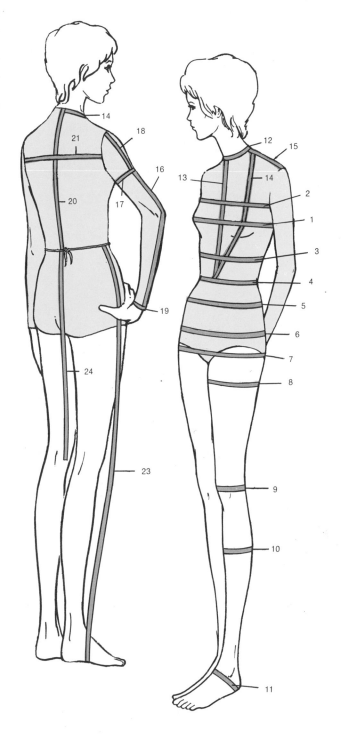

Ease

Ease means freedom from constraint, and *wearing ease* has been built into all Vogue Patterns to insure your comfort and mobility. Understanding your body contour will help you achieve a perfect fit. *Style ease,* on the other hand, is fullness added beyond the wearing ease needs and is an integral part of some garment designs.

WEARING EASE: A garment made exactly to your measurements would restrict body movement and ride up—the bodice would bind and pull across the bust and back, the skirt would cup under the buttocks, and you would not be able to sit down comfortably. Wearing ease has been calculated by experts from the standard body measurements listed on the envelope for your pattern size. Never plan to use the wearing ease for a specific style to accommodate body circumference. If your measurements do not correspond to those on the pattern envelope, adjust your pattern to achieve a comfortable fit. A great aid to fitting problems can be found in "Vogue's Guide to Perfect Fit of Fitted Garments;" using this special pattern, you can work out your personal measurements and figure needs as well as test to find the wearing ease you require. Books II and III give details on personalizing this pattern.

The accompanying chart approximates the wearing ease in Vogue Patterns' fitted garment shell beyond the actual body circumference measurements for each figure type. These measurements apply only to the close fit found in the fitting shell and will vary when related to the other garment styles that are available to you.

	Misses' Miss Petite		Women's	Half Size
Bust	3″	3″	3½″	3½″
Waist (dress)	¾″	¾″	1″	¾″
Waist (skirt)	½″	½″	¾″	½″
Full Hip	2″	2″	2¾″	2½″

Caution: In Vogue Patterns, the wearing ease may not always be exactly the same because it is affected by style. Halter-neck, strapless, and extremely cut-away armhole styles in which the bodice must be supported by the body to stay in place, have minimal ease allowed beyond the standard circumference measurements. Suggested fabrics affect considerations of wearing ease. Patterns designed "For Stretchable Unbonded Knits" or "For Two-Way Stretch Knits" have less wearing ease because the elasticity of the fabric will contribute to a comfortable, flattering fit.

Personal Preference: Some women do not feel comfortable wearing clothes fitted closely to the body, while others are not happy unless they look like they have been poured into their garments; often women with excellent figures and grooming will gladly sacrifice comfort to achieve a lithe, streamlined look. Excessively close fit exaggerates figure faults, and most fabrics cannot withstand the strain. Heavier women should use wearing ease to smooth over midriff bulge or heavy upper arms, and to avoid bursting seams. Do not choose a smaller pattern size because you plan to use the style ease for wearing ease—everything in the pattern is proportionally smaller and you may distort the designer's intended silhouette.

If you prefer closely fitted garments, choose patterns described on the envelope back as being fitted or semi-fitted. Never choose a fashion that has design fullness or style ease, only to fit it out and destroy the look and line of the garment.

YOUR SHAPE: The devices of camouflage used in fashion are based on principles of art and design. In considering body weight, optical illusion often comes into play. Many women appear to be either on the heavy or the thin side; even women of medium weight can, by their height, create the illusion of more or less bulk. We at Vogue Patterns believe, after carefully considering statistics relating to the number of figure variations possible, that *height* is the most important element to be used when trying to disguise a figure flaw or to enhance a good feature; however, bone structure, weight, and individual features also influence one's bulk.

Due to the interrelationship of height and the illusion of bulk, a *heavy* woman would do well to emphasize vertical lines; a princess line will elongate her body. Horizontal styling, such as yokes or gathered skirts, would increase visual bulk. Kimono, dolman, or sleeves with ruffles lead the eye disadvantageously across a full bust or hip area. Choosing gabrics in subtle, cool colors—the green-violet-blue family—will diminish bulk, as will fabrics with smooth textures and matte finishes.

The woman who is *thin* is flattered by soft fabrics and blousy styles; she would do well to avoid shifts and straight lines. The layered look is made to order for her. A woman with a thin, bony figure should avoid fashions combining clingy fabrics with body-fitting styles. Usually it is wise to cover thin arms or legs. Fabrics in warm, bright colors—red-orange-yellow—and nubby or shiny surfaces will tend to increase size. Women who are short as well as thin are advised to choose prints and textures that are in scale with their bone structure and individual features. The object is to pad out the figure by using texture, style fullness, and color. Vertical lines are in order for a heightening effect. The Vogue Sewing Book (pages 14–31) deals specifically with colors, lines, and style details which are appropriate for various figures.

After combining style and fabric in a fashion which will enhance your figure, it is up to you to fit your clothes to further disguise or flatter your individual contours. If you are heavy, remember to leave enough ease across those areas that will be subjected to the most strain—hips, bust, biceps, etc.—and avoid clingy fabrics. In general, a fleshy figure requires more wearing ease than a bony figure.

SILHOUETTES: The overall shape of a garment is referred to as its silhouette. The "look" or shape of fashion changes noticeably every fifteen or twenty years, often in reflection of the contemporary society and its values. Bustles and mini-skirts, though very different in silhouette, were both a product of their times and were designed to flatter the wearer. You can choose from among the current silhouettes those that best express who you are and what you would like to enhance or hide.

There is challenge in store as you choose the silhouette that does the most for your figure as you have evaluated it. Although many variations exist within each category, there are four basic silhouettes from which the designer can evolve a particular fashion point of view: the fitted garment, the semi-fitted garment, the slightly fitted garment, and the loosely fitted garment. Each of these silhouettes may be incorporated into a different part of a single garment as well. Later on, you will see that many shapes are evolved from others by simply adding fullness; the designer controls the silhouette by the amount of fullness added or taken away. Once a pattern has been made, the seamstress should not attempt to change its basic silhouette. It is important to be familiar with the appearance and characteristic fit of each shape.

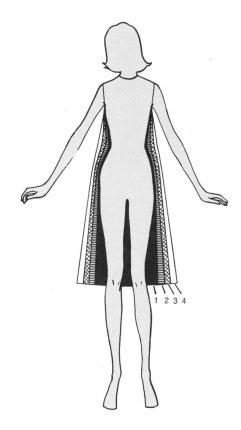

1 2 3 4

A *fitted* garment follows your natural curves; its wearing ease may also be its style ease. When fitted too closely, it will reveal your figure and the outline of undergarments in detail, and wrinkle easily. A well-fitting garment of this type will touch the body without constraint or exaggeration (1).

A *semi-fitted* garment fits smoothly over the bust and slightly loose at waist and hips. Some style ease is used for each area. Women with slight figure faults can rely on this silhouette (2).

A *slightly fitted* garment barely follows the body shape and has considerable style ease. It is an excellent silhouette to select for disguising figure flaws (3).

A *loosely fitted* garment has much style ease and only hints at body contour. The fullness begins above the bustline and falls loosely around the body. There is considerable coverage with loosely fitted garments, but heavier figures would do well to avoid them because they do convey a feeling of volume (4).

FASHION VARIATIONS: Well-planned fashion designs are guided by the four basic fitted silhouettes, but the variations are limitless. Few of us would want a wardrobe of only pure shapes. The refinements of these shapes—high fit, waist fit, hip fit, and bias fit—offer the widest choice of figure-flattering fashions.

The description *high fit* indicates a close fit through and just under the bust area. This should not suggest to you that the rest of the garment will be fitted too: the designer may add style ease 2″ or more below the bust for a body-skimming skirt, while incorporating it with a raised-waist, seamed, or fitted Empire bodice. A princess-seamed dress or a darted sheath can give you the same subtle styling.

In *waist fit,* sometimes a midriff inset is fashion's current focus. Styles that require close fit in the waist area can have a bodice and skirt gathered into a waistline stay, or can be tucked or darted. By *hip fit* we mean close fit in the hip area. Dropped-waist seams immediately come to mind, but a classic shirt dress with a loosely fitted bodice may have a straight skirt that is hip fitted. Hip-yoked skirts and pants, and skirts or dresses with stitched pleats fall into this category, too.

Perennial favorites are *bias-cut* garments. These can be made to fit perfectly without a seam or dart for shaping. A dress can mold smoothly over bust or hips no matter how much style ease exists. Important *geometric* seaming details—horizontal, vertical, asymmetrical, and curved—are another design tactic. Realizing the design possibilities inherent in combining and varying all of these features should give you an insight into the resources of a designer. After familiarizing yourself with these, you will be able to successfully combine visual knowledge with the description of silhouette found on the envelope of every Vogue Pattern.

Judging the shape of a dress from an illustration or photograph can be misleading. A skirt that seems slightly A-line might actually be wider. As accurate as a pattern illustration is, there is much latitude in your interpretation of what you see. An accurate guide to visualizing the shape of your garment is printed on the back of your pattern envelope under the title *Width at Lower Edge.* This measurement of the fullness of the skirt or the width of a pant leg is an all-around measurement; to "see" the actual width of the garment in your mind's eye when selecting a pattern, compare these measurements with those of clothes you already own. Visualize half the number of inches of the stated width at lower edge while studying the illustration. The front or back of a garment may have more or less sweep due to styling (pleats or panels). In this case, use the all-around measurement indicated on the pattern envelope as a rough guide.

The *fabrics* which you select may determine whether a silhouette will flatter you. Color, texture, weight, and scale of a printed or structural motif are decisive. Sometimes when two identical styles have been made in different fabrics—one a plain color, and the other a print—you would expect them both to have the same fashion impact. But when worn, something happens between you, the style, and the fabric . . . the plain one can be smashing while the print may seem busy and unflattering (or the reverse). The perfect combination comes easier for some, but with experience, you will learn instinctively what will work for you.

So far we have considered the points you should cover in working toward a well-fitting dress. Now let us consider some other garment types in relation to wearing ease, style ease, and the four basic silhouettes. *Blouses* would be fitted the same as a dress with this exception—if they are to be worn over skirt or pants, you must allow ease for this extra layer. *Skirts* always have waist fit, due to the application of a waist-line finish. In the case of hip huggers, they have hip fit.

Pants in any length—from ankle to short shorts—vary in leg fullness. This style ease takes many forms—whether skirt-like or a fashion variation like knickers. Classic pants have waist and hip fit; as style ease increases, only waist fit may survive. Jumpsuits fit like the dress and pants combination from which they are derived.

Wearing ease has been carefully built into every Vogue Patterns *outerwear* design. Jackets will fit smoothly over a dress or blouse that is not extremely bulky. Coats will fit over a jacket. When a pattern has a jacket that is a cut-off version of a coat, the two cannot be worn one over the other. Fit a jacket or coat over the garments with which they will be worn—read the description on the pattern envelope back. A two-piece dress top may look like a jacket, but it will not fit like one. The fitting of outer-wear is discussed on page 77. See page 78 for a bulky lining.

Pattern Check-out

Even if you are an accomplished seamstress and are certain that your pattern size is correct, it will always be to your advantage to compare the measurements of your fashion pattern with your perfected basic fitted pattern. If fitting was not begun before you cut your fabric, there is often little that can be done to correct major errors. Obviously, it is impossible to add more fabric to a garment which is too small. A garment which requires extensive removal of fabric risks style and grain distortion. Do not forget to incorporate your knowledge of wearing ease and style ease (page 24), and the character of your fashion fabric in your evaluation of the measurements you will take.

Having made a master pattern from *Vogue's Guide to Perfect Fit of Fitted Garments* and your perfected muslin, you can accomplish any pattern check easily. If A-line styles (without a waist seam) are your favorite, it may be simpler to use your personally adjusted *Vogue's Guide to Perfect Fit of A-line Garments* as your master pattern. Determine which portion of your body circumference the pattern pieces represent. Depending on the style, fashion pattern pieces may represent a whole or half of a garment section in circumference, as well as varying amounts of the garment's total length. This will have great bearing on how the pattern pieces are to be measured and evaluated. Slide your master pattern under the fashion pattern, aligning the centers vertically and waistlines horizontally. Note how your fashion pattern accommodates your body size, wearing ease, and style ease, as well as your specific body contours. It is through the use of seams, darts, tucks, pleats, and gathers that two-dimensional fabric becomes a three-dimensional garment.

When measuring pattern pieces, you must include only the garment proper—exclude all pleat underlays, overlapping edges, seam and dart allowances, etc. You can pin the pattern pieces together like the garment and measure as a unit, or you can measure each piece from center or seamline to seamline and add these individual measurements. When measuring pattern bodice bust circumference, place the tape just above the bust darts. Add together the measurements necessary to arrive at a total garment circumference or length. Compare these sums to your body measurements; keep in mind wearing ease, style ease, fabric character, and the bulk of internal construction details. Then make any changes in the pattern that you have found to be necessary.

The **bodice** area is crucial to fit. Think about the type of garment you are making, the bust fit, the style ease, and the wearing ease. Remember, when measuring the waist, a thick torso needs more wearing ease than an hour-glass figure. Then check the neck, bust, and waist circumference along with the lengths.

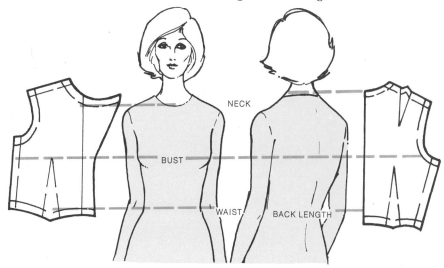

Sleeves require careful measuring. To evaluate your wearing ease needs, measure your bicep relaxed; then make a fist and flex your muscle and measure again. This will give you an idea of how much wearing ease you will need over your actual bicep measurement. Heavier arms need more wearing ease than thin arms. Fabric has an effect, too—tightly woven fabrics will not, of course, give as much as a knit fabric will.

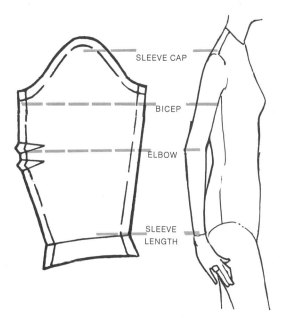

Skirts need the same consideration for the waist fit as does the bodice, but your needs for high and full hip are especially critical. Making sure you have the right hip fit in the exact spot is essential since, once your fabric is cut out, you may not have the fabric you need for a comfortable and attractive fit.

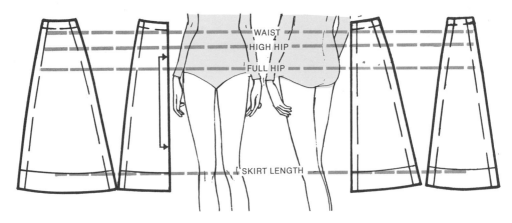

The cronic problems of fitting *pants* can be somewhat eliminated when measuring the pattern before you cut into your fashion fabric. Waist, high hip, and full hip can never be fitted adequately if you haven't allowed for your curves in the right places in your fabric. The same goes for thigh bulge, large buttocks, and other figure flaws. If you haven't made a fitting muslin for pants, you should do so now to eliminate the guesswork of fitting pants once and for all. Then fabric will be your only remaining consideration—tightly woven, firm fabrics do not give as much as knits.

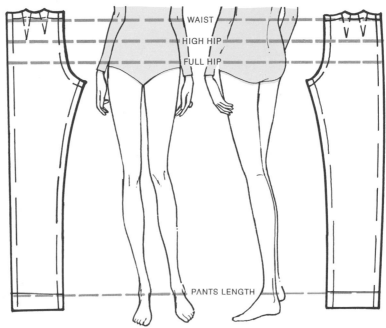

Fabrics . . . And You

The woman who sews is a sensual woman—whether she knows it or not. She finds fabrics irresistable, exciting, and habit-forming. In closets, on shelves, and in drawers throughout the land, a woman's personal collection of fabrics awaits her special touch. Sometimes, on impulse at a sale or after careful shopping and consideration, a woman will purchase a fabric she loves. Later, when home, she discovers that she was simply infatuated or that she really cannot find the time to sew. And so the hoard of fabric continues to grow and, along with it, the feeling that she is never free, that she is possessed.

Covering the body for warmth and decoration is human instinct. We have been knitting, weaving, or binding fibers together to make body coverings for ages. From the beginning, textiles have existed for two reasons: aesthetics and performance. It is no wonder, then, that the woman who sews is driven by deep personal and cultural needs to possess the beauty and function of fabric.

Why, then, does the creative, fabric-loving seamstress balk when we try to tell her something about the science of textiles? There is interest when we talk about natural organic dyes made of juniper or sage brush brewed over an open fire by Navaho weavers. But talk about polyesters, or crimping, or dimensional stability and the interest is gone—technology seems to intimidate some of us.

Character

The woman who sews is interested in sewability—slipperiness and stiffness are some characteristics which would make a fabric difficult to sew without consideration of its function beforehand. There are times when stiffness or slipperiness is a desirable trait, such as in interfacings, linings, or underlinings. Then these fabrics are sought out for the very characteristics that otherwise limit their use.

Fabrics today have many traits that make them individual. These characteristics in and of themselves are neither good nor bad—they are simply characteristics. If a fabric is used in a garment where the characteristics of the fabric answer the functions of the garment, all is well. If the woman who sews fights against those natural characteristics, the fit and the function of the garment will be impaired.

The woman who sews does not have to be an expert on each fabric she uses, but certainly an over-all familiarity with fabrics and their physical and chemical characteristics is essential. Here are characteristics with which you should be concerned:

Luster: Does it have a sheen?

Recovery: Will it stretch and recover?

Resiliency: Will the fabric return to its original shape when stretched?

Drapability: How does it fall?

Heat Conductivity: Does it retain or release body heat?

Porosity: Is the weave open to allow air circulation or to absorb moisture?

Washability: Can it be laundered? How?

Absorbency (or Hydrophilic Properties): How fast is body moisture absorbed and then evaporated?

Affinity for Dyes: Will it take color well? Will it bleed? Is it colorfast?

Sunlight, Mildew, Atmospheric Pollutants: How is it affected by these?

Dimensional Stability: Will it shrink?

31

Bleachability: Will it "yellow" or "gray" with use? Can you bleach it?
Non-irritating: Does it scratch?
Durable Press: Can it be laundered and not require subsequent ironing?
Soil Release: Does it resist soiling?

Stain Resistant: Does it resist water- or oil-born stains?
No-cling: Does it resist clinging or the build-up of static electricity?
Bonding or Laminating: Is it permanent?
Heat: Will pressing scorch or melt it?

Once you have learned to look for these traits, you will realize how important it is to read hang-tags, labels, and descriptions on bolt ends when shopping for fabrics.

HAND AND DRAPE: The creative seamstress is deeply concerned with how her fabric will look and how it will perform once it becomes a garment: She cares how it feels and how it will hang. All these things affect the fit of the garment immeasurably. The way the fabric feels to the touch is called the *hand* of the fabric. The way it hangs and falls into soft or crisp folds is called the *drape* of the fabric.

SOFT

CRISP

In order to fit your garments to professional standards, it is essential to know and get along with the "personality" of each fabric with which you work. The individual characteristics of each and every fabric are integrally related to its content and construction. If you understand some of the reasons why the fabric you adore might be termed difficult, you will be better able to handle it.

Choosing the correct fabric is perhaps the most critical decision you must make when embarking on a sewing project. Always buy quality fabrics, for the time and effort put into a sewing project will always justify the initial expense. However, quality fabric cannot always be determined by price; you must also learn to judge fabrics by touching them. Although experience will be your best teacher in choosing fabrics, you will find that The Vogue Sewing Book (pages 32–81) contains valuable information.

Your reaction when you touch a fabric is often a true response to the character of that fabric. We know instinctively that when a fabric is *soft,* it will fall easily and gracefully. The touch of a *crisp* fabric tells you clearly that here is substance and stature that must be dealt with firmly. In this way, the hand of a fabric tells you what can be done with it.

Everything about the fabric influences its softness and crispness. Some fibers are, by nature, more supple and pliable than others. When made into different yarns, the same fiber can seem soft or crisp, depending on the character and weight of the yarn. Fabric constructions—weaving, knitting, etc.—and finishes also influence the hand of the fabric. If the fabric is loosely woven, it will usually be a soft fabric, but this does not imply that tightly woven fabrics are always crisp. Think of the soft, supple crepes that are made of tightly woven silk. Neither the fiber nor weight of a fabric determines crispness or softness. Silk is soft, resilient, and can be woven into taffeta, shantung, or ottoman—all of which are crisp. Cotton can be woven into fabrics as delicate as a Swiss handkerchief or strong enough to sail a boat.

Challis is lightweight and soft, but organza is lightweight and crisp. Medium weight flannel is soft, but medium weight garbardine is crisp. Textures and raised surfaces, whether classic or novelty, add yet another facet to the personality of a fabric. Though they all have raised surfaces, terry cloths and velours are soft, whereas brocades and jacquards are crisp. Obviously fiber, yarn, fabric construction, and finishes all have much to do with hand, and no factor is more important than another.

After you have chosen your fabric wisely you can be assured of two things—that it will be flattering and functional. The key to fitting garments that are constructed of soft or crisp fabric lies in what you already know. The woman who sews has built up a repertoire of sewing and pressing techniques upon which she relies. She knows about laying out patterns and about cutting and marking fabrics. She knows construction and pressing techniques, and the care needed in cleaning garments. It is then a matter of generalizing this particularized information in terms of fitting. In construction, if a fabric is loosely woven, it is apt to ravel and stretch. It will require additional support, protection, and finishing. When fitting a fabric that has a tendency to ravel or stretch, minimal handling, marking, pinning, and pressing are recommended. Conversely, when fitting a hard-finish fabric that can take much handling and will not stretch easily, you can mark, pin, and press without worry. If you apply your intuition and interrelate what you know already, you will discover that you really understand a lot about fitting delicate or firm, soft or crisp fabrics.

When fitting a soft fabric like lawn, challis, chiffon, or a lingerie knit, the style and the function of the garment will determine the required amount of ease. Soft fabrics tend to cling, even though this may not be dictated by the garment style. Do not over-fit a soft fabric since it may be fragile; undue stress on the seams of this type of fabric causes them to pull out and fray. In sheers or silk crepes, beware of leaving pin marks during fitting. Mark your garment carefully so that if the seamlines or darts must be moved, you will not have indelible markings on your garment. When underlining, do not try to change the characteristics of the fabric by combining a soft fabric with a stiff underlining as ridges will show through. A soft, tightly woven underlining of the same weight or lighter should add stability to a soft fashion fabric. Underlining must be compatible with the fabric with which it will be used.

When fitting a crisp fabric like garbardine, denim, piqué, linen, or a bonded fabric, you will find that because the fabric stands out from the body and falls into firm folds, it is most suited for use in body-skimming styles that are not fit close to the body. Design with architectural fullness and springy pleats, rather than soft gathers and folds, are best for crisp fabrics. In crisp fabrics of medium to heavy weights, you will find that even more ease may be needed. On satins, vinyls, or leather-like fabrics, place pins only within the seam allowances throughout all phases of cutting, fitting, and construction. If both a fabric and your pattern's style lines are new to you, you may wish to make a fitting muslin first. Do not, as you fit the actual garment, do any marking or pinning that will cause permanent damage.

FABRIC LAYERS: When making a garment that has an underlining, interfacing, interlining, lining, or a combination of these, you will be faced with fitting two or more fabric layers smoothly over one another. Think of the component fabrics as concentric circles; the outermost layer—the fashion fabric—must have just enough extra ease to mold smoothly over the inner layers and your body. Each inner layer must be slightly smaller than the next outer one. A pattern which includes individual pattern pieces for these internal fabrics has built-in ease for layering.

The weight, hand, and surface texture of a fabric will also affect the fit of each layer. For example, even though a pattern calls for and has been designed to accommodate a lining, your choice of a thick, furry fabric; a slippery, crisp satin; or a pliant, soft crepe will have great influence on the refinement of the fit of your garment. Similarly a toothy or a smooth underlining or interfacing, and a napped or flat interlining will have some bearing on the way in which the layers will fit over one another. Again, we stress that the differences in the circumferences of these layers are very slight—but crucial to perfect fabric fit.

Underlining is cut from the same pattern pieces as your fashion fabric; the two layers are then handled as one throughout the garment construction (see page 59 for fitting with underlining). Underlining lengthens the life of the garment and prevents interior construction details from showing through. The underlining is usually lighter and softer than your fashion fabric.

Underlining should be chosen by testing it with your fashion fabric. Drape the two together over your hand and make sure that their characters are compatible with one another. The style of your garment might dictate the need for underlining in two weights. Perhaps a soft batiste underlining in a drapey bodice and a lightweight organza underlining for a fully gathered skirt would be appropriate for the silhouette you wish to achieve. Of course, it is your prerogative to use no underlining for that same gathered skirt, but expect the drape and bounce of the skirt to be less perky. Underlined fashions frequently are quite resistant to wilting during wearings.

Batiste, China silk, and marquisette are lightweight, and are good choice for underlining crepe, voile, cottons, blends, and lightweight wools. For wool coatings suitings, and brocades, use a medium to heavyweight underlining like muslin, organdy, or a lightweight interfacing. There also are many commercial underlinings that come in a great variety of weights and fashion colors.

Interfacing gives body and durability in garment areas that must retain their crispness and shape. In loungewear, lingerie, or swimwear, a soft or high-loft interfacing can be used to ensure lasting shape in the bust area. Interfacing is available in woven or non-woven types, and comes soft or crisp in weights ranging from light to heavy. Some non-woven interfacings that are made to stretch in all directions are called all-bias. Press-on interfacing reinforces and increases durability, but once applied, tends to restrict the suppleness of the fabric. Make no fitting changes after it is applied. Hair canvas is recommended for couture dressmaking and tailoring. It comes in different weights and qualities, shapes beautifully, and retains its flexibility.

Interfacing should be compatible with the outer fabric—drape the two fabrics together to test as you did for underlining. Within a garment, it is possible to use interfacing of one weight for a collar, and interfacing of other weights in the cuffs, pocket flaps, and front edges. Generally, interfacing should be lighter in weight than the outer fashion fabric. For a special purpose, you might select an interfacing that will dramatically change the performance of the fabric in a small section of the garment; this practice should not be used indiscriminately or thoughtlessly.

Interlining is added to outerwear for additional warmth. Fabric for this must be chosen carefully because it should not interfere with the drape of the fashion fabric or with the garment silhouette intended by the designer. Because many interlinings are of bulky, high-loft fabrics, their affect on garment fit is quite pronounced—be judicious in making your fabric selection. If your garment must be interlined, yet you do not, when wearing it, want to present a cumbersome figure, choose an interlining fabric that is somewhat smooth—like lamb's wool—rather than one that is extremely bulky. Interlining is handled as one with the lining fabric in fitting, just as the underlining is handled with the fashion fabric. Fit these lining layers before you fit your fashion garment; see page 78 for handling bulky linings. When cutting, always allow wider seam allowances in the fashion fabric for extra ease.

Lining provides a couture finish for the interior of your fashion. The ideal lining fabrics are soft, light in weight, slippery, and opaque. The additional bulk presented by such a lining is minimal, yet it will have a subtle, persistent influence on the fit of the fabric layers which are outside it. Linings are customarily fitted in the finished garment, but their impending presence must be considered throughout all stages of fitting and construction, as well as in the selection of appropriate fabrics.

For detailed information on alternative fabrics for interfacings, underlinings, interlinings, and linings, refer to pages 80–85 of The Vogue Sewing Book.

FITTING SPECIFICS: Technology has created fabrics which never existed before or which are up-to-date modifications of old favorites. They often demand special methods of cutting, marking, sewing, and pressing. Vogue Patterns has created a series of booklets to inform you of the techniques particularly suited to these fabrics. It is essential that you understand the construction demands of these fabrics to effectively evaluate and apply fitting techniques to them. On the following pages is a chart which will aid you in sorting out many of the details pertaining to these fabrics which may have some, or considerable, influence on your approach to fitting them.

The Fitting Dimensions

Fabric and Fiber	Characteristics	Preparation
Bias-Cut Fabrics Fiber: Wool, cotton, silk, linen, rayon, synthetics, blends	Soft or crisp; woven fabrics on true bias run along 45° angle formed when the warp and weft are at right angles to each other; folds gracefully; hand depends on fabric; molds to figure; eases well; some can take soft drapey styles; stretches easily.	Work on a smooth surface and support fabric while cutting. Make seam allowances 1½″ wide on vertical seams. Do not remove pattern pieces until you are ready for construction. Store flat.
Bias Designs Fiber: Cotton, wool, silk, rayon, synthetics, blends	Soft or crisp; woven or knits; fabric often cannot be straightened when design is printed rather than woven.	Handle as you would any stable fabric; follow knits for bias design knits. Uneven plaids may not match.
Brocades (embossed) Fiber: Cotton, wool, silk, synthetics, blends	Crisp; raised designs, some are reversible (either side can be used). Ravels, metal threads may tarnish, pins may break metallic threads.	Follow a "With Nap" layout. Avoid using a tracing wheel. Make all markings on underlining.
Crepes, Satin-Like Fabrics (ciré), **Soft Sheers** (chiffon) Fiber: Silk, rayon, wool, synthetics	Soft; supple; falls in soft folds; ravels easily; pins and needles mar surface of fabric; handle as little as possible.	Follow a "With Nap" layout if shading is evident. Do not use a tracing wheel; test chalk or pencil before using. Mark lightly. Use sharp scissors.
Durable Press Fabrics— due to fiber or finish Fiber: Cotton, linen, some wool, rayon, nylon, polyester, blends	Soft or crisp; requires little or no ironing. Grease spots are hard to remove, so look for soil-release properties; watch grain and print as it can't be straightened—the finish sets threads.	Avoid placing pattern on center fold if it has a crease which will not press out. Watch out for distorted grain or print; align grainline with selvages or fold, and cut as it came off the bolt.
Easy Care Fabrics—due to fiber or finish Fiber: Cotton, wool, silk, nylon, polyester, triacetate, blends	Soft or crisp; woven or knit; requires little or no ironing; machine washable, but can shrink in dryer—best drip-dried. Usually washable, wrinkle-resistant.	Follow standard knits, woven or durable press techniques

# of Fashion Fabrics

Construction	Pressing	Fitting
Staystitch neck and armhole edges. Do not over-handle. Easing is accomplished quite simply. Use strips of tissue paper to prevent stretching of seams during construction.	Follow fabric type pressing techniques. Always test; use steam carefully. Do not press along the bias—press along the straight grain whenever possible. Press with light pressure and never slide the iron across the fabric.	Before fitting, hang the basted garment for 24 hours; darts and pockets may have to be re-marked. Do not over-fit as this will weaken the garment due to the bias "hanging out." Puckering can be eliminated by opening the seam and easing out the excess. Use lining or underlining at stress points (derrière, elbows). Underline bias collars. Darts can be worked out of a design during fittings if desired.
Let the fabric dictate your construction. See: Crisp, Durable Press, Easy Care, Hard Finish, Knits, Napped.	Let the fabric dictate pressing technique to use.	Let the fabric determine how much fitting you do. Do not over-fit, as motif may be distorted.
Clean-finish seams or line garment. Make facings of lining fabric if heavy or scratchy.	Use a press pad to protect raised designs. Test on a swatch. Press lightly, using no steam. Careless pressing may wilt the fabric.	Avoid pin fittings—make a muslin garment first. Avoid over-handling. Overlap seam allowances to baste for a fitting.
Tape shoulder, neck, or other seams that may support the garment. Use a fine needle, and adjust stitch size, tension, and pressure. Never re-stitch seams in fabrics that mar.	Test effects of steam—it can cause permanent puckers. Use a dry press cloth. Press gently on wrong side; do not press over pins. Baste with a fine needle and silk thread.	Do not over-fit—taper adjustments gradually into original markings. Watch out for pin marks. Make a test muslin for fabrics that mar.
Keep seams from puckering by holding fabric taut when stitching. Straight seams require more care than slightly shaped ones. Pre-shrink zippers in hot water.	Sleeve cap ease will not shrink when pressed—eliminate some ease before cutting out the pattern.	Seams cannot be let out, as marks are usually permanent; make a muslin if fit of silhouette is unknown to you. Do not over-fit—seams may pull out.
Same as for knits, durable press, and wovens.	Some behave like durable press, some like knits.	Let the fabric structure dictate the fitting technique you need—some will be fit like knits, others like durable press.

Fabric and Fiber	Characteristics	Preparation
Furs Fiber: Rabbit, lamb, opposum, skunk, seal, mouton, pony	Soft or crisp; curly furs (lamb) swirl and have no nap; straight-haired furs (rabbit) have nap and should be worked lengthwise; short, stiff, straight-haired furs (pony) have more pronounced hair pattern. Old fur has dry, weakened skin. When seams are abutted and stitched, the seamline is covered by the furry surface. The edges will not ravel.	Lay out pattern pieces with the grain. Leave no seam allowances on most furs; seams are abutted. Furs with soft skins can be cut with ¼″ seams.
Fur-Like Fabrics Fiber: Modacrylics	Same as for fur. Knit backing may be scratchy and stiff.	Lay out pattern pieces with the grain. Make sure to include seam allowances when cutting.
Hard Finish Fabrics (sailcloth, canvas, covert, denim, gabardine, duck) Fiber: Wool, cotton, synthetics, blends	Crisp; falls in stiff folds; durable, long-wearing, resists wrinkling.	Be sure your shears are sharp. To mark, use tracing wheel and dressmaker's tracing paper, or chalk and pins.
Knits (stretch, rib, stretch lace, tricot, double knit, raschel) Fiber: Cotton, wool, silk, nylon, acrylic, rayon, polyester, modacrylic, other synthetics, blends	Soft or crisp; smooth, silky, loopy, nubby, ribbed, or bulky. Stable knits have minimum stretch and recovery; moderately stable knits can cling or stretch. Stretchable knits have much give and are used over body contours in a stretched condition. Knits stretch most along crosswise grain (called course), and therefore have no real bias. Knits have a wale instead of lengthwise grain.	Support is required. Most patterns can be used for stable knits. Use patterns specifically designed for stretchable unbonded knits. Add to side seam allowances on stretchable knits for fitting. Use a "With Nap" layout because most knits have shading. A tracing wheel can damage lightweight knits.
Laminates (knits, crepes, laces, woolens) Fiber: Cotton, wool, synthetics; laminated with foam or adhesive to tricot or other backing	Crisp—more so than same fabric prior to lamination. Beware of laminates that separate; watch grain—once bonded off-grain, the fabric cannot be straightened; cut as it is. Sometimes has tendency to ravel.	Use sharp scissors and be alert to grain distortion on right side of fabric.

Construction	Pressing	Fitting
Cut edges are whipstitched together and reinforced with tape. Furs with soft skin can be straight or zigzag stitched.	Never press directly on the fur. On thick edges, pounding with a mallet is helpful in flattening.	It is essential to make a felt or muslin trial garment. When fitting, use long strips of 1″ wide masking tape on skin side. Fur that has thin skin can be pinned or basted sparingly, using ¼″ seams. Reinforce seams with tape as soon as possible. Do not over-fit or trim darts until fit has been finalized. When wearing fur as a lining, use wider seam allowances in outer fabric layers to go over the fur.
Seams and seam finishes will vary, depending on fabric type. Seams can be abutted or range from ⅛″-⅝″. Trim hairs from fur side of seam allowance when fit has been finalized. Line the garment if fabric is scratchy.	Same as for furs.	A felt or muslin trial garment is recommended. Do not trim fur from seam allowances until fit has been finalized. Seams can be pinned or basted for fitting.
Choose simple styles which require no easing because fullness can not be shrunk out.	Use steam but always test on a swatch first. On covert and worsted, use a press cloth. You may need to use a pounder and a point presser to get creased edges and flat seams.	Can take handling, but staystitch curves. When pin fitting, place pins close together. When basting, backstitch every 2″-3″.
Use a ball point needle if necessary (#14 for medium to heavyweight, #11 for lightweight). Adjust stitch length to 12-15 per inch; balance tension. Or, use a narrow zigzag. Adjust presser foot so top and bottom fabrics feed evenly. Use polyester or cotton-covered polyester thread. Seam finishes usually are unnecessary because there is little ravelling. Stay edges and seams like the shoulder and neck.	Do not use steam unless you have tested its effects. Use a press cloth when pressing from the right side; use a low temperature and press with the lengthwise wale to avoid stretching.	They should fit like woven fabrics. Baste stretchable knits (see page 48). Strive for body-hugging effect at curves and contours on fitted garments. Wrinkles can be caused in seams by faulty stitching. Usually a knit garment that does not fit looks either baggy or constraining, rather than wrinkled and pulled as a woven would look.
Reduce bulk in seam and darts by trimming and grading. A self-fabric facing may be too bulky; interfacing can be eliminated; do not underline. Adjust stitch size, tension, and pressure. Seam finishes may be unnecessary.	Test fabric for shrinkage and pressing techniques. Beware of using too much heat on tricot side of fabric. Use a press cloth.	Over-fitting causes wrinkles; leave in enough wearing ease. Do not over-handle near delicate seam allowances. Do not slash darts until fit has been finalized.

Fabric and Fiber	Characteristics	Preparation
Leathers, Suedes, Leather-Like Fabrics Fiber: Leather and suede; tanned hide of animal used face up or down; vinyl (plastic with or without knit backing)	Soft or crisp; may be smooth, textured, or grainy. Suede is napped. Vinyl is smooth, grained, or embossed. Leather is porous, stretchy, has grain. Vinyl is non-porous and cracks. Keep rolled for storage.	Follow a "With Nap" layout. Use a razor blade to cut single layers if leather; some leather-likes can be cut with scissors. Use weights or tape; do not pin garment area.
Metallics, Novelty Fabrics (beads, sequins) Fiber: Metal threads, beads or sequins in or on synthetics, silk, or wool fabrics.	Soft or crisp; clinging or stable; may be scratchy; metal may crack or peel. Many ravel considerably.	Use special shears or ones you can discard, as cutting dulls them. Pin in seam allowances so metal threads are not damaged. Mark with chalk; do not use a tracing wheel.
Napped Fabrics (flannel, melton, fleece, camel hair); **Pile Fabrics** (corduroy, velvet, velour, terry cloth) Fiber: Wool, cotton, rayon, synthetics, blends	Soft or crisp; textured, brushed, specially woven, bulky, flat, differing in weight and texture. Color is richer with pile up.	Use a "With Nap" layout. Cut single layer at a time if fabric is thick. Mark with tailor's tacks; baste with silk thread or transfer all marks to underlining.
Plaids, Stripes Fiber: Cotton, wool, silk, synthetics, rayon, blends	Soft or crisp, depending on fabric, construction, weight, and fiber. Plaids and stripes must be matched. Even plaids and balanced stripes are easiest to match.	Use a "With Nap" layout for an uneven plaid or unbalanced stripe; match vertically and horizontally if possible. See also The Vogue Sewing Book (pages 172-179). Cutting on bias may involve changing grainline.
Prints (large-scale, border) Fiber: Cotton, wool, silk, linen, synthetics, blends	Soft or crisp, depending on fabric, construction, weight, and fiber.	Place pattern so fabric design is shown to advantage. Match one-way designs. Eliminate seams for border prints if possible; plan hem before cutting. Follow a "With Nap" layout. See The Vogue Sewing Book, page 180.
Ribs (ottoman); **Diagonals** (obvious twills, herringbone) Fiber: Cotton, wool, silk, rayon, synthetics, blends	Soft or crisp; falls in stiff folds. Rib or diagonal is part of the fabric structure.	Follow pattern recommendations; do not use a pattern whose design lines oppose the diagonal like raglan, kimono, or V-neck would. Match ribs if they are 1/4″ or wider.
Stretch Fabrics Fibers: Synthetics, blends of natural and synthetic fibers	Soft or crisp; stretchy, elastic. One- or two-way stretch; woven or knitted with resilient fibers; some garments call for lengthwise stretch (pants, jumpsuits).	Spread fabric taut, then let it relax on a smooth surface before cutting. Lay out pattern directionally, making best use of fabric stretch. Use sharp pins and shears.

Construction	Pressing	Fitting
Use V-shaped leather needles on sewing machine. Leather, suede, and vinyl will stretch but do not ease readily.	Seams can be glued, then hammered flat, and the glue removed.	Make a muslin or felt trial garment; make all adjustments and alterations before you cut garment. Use paper clips to try on garments. Do not pin—this will puncture the surface.
Use a fine needle and synthetic thread. Avoid making pin marks and re-stitching seams. Clean-finish seams, and line metallic brocade garments that are scratchy.	Test on a swatch, using no steam; it may dull, tarnish, or melt beads, sequins, or metallic threads. Press lightly.	Pin only inside seam allowances or, lap seams and baste. Avoid over-handling. Do not over-fit as it may crack at the wrinkles caused by tight fit.
Baste with silk thread, back-stitching every 2″-3″ before stitching. Decrease machine pressure and stitch with the nap, holding fabric taut. Use a fine needle and 10-12 stitches per inch.	Press with a light hand. Use a self-fabric press cloth, and a needle board or terry cloth pressing surface. A flattened pile or nap cannot be restored.	Do not over-fit; texture will be distorted. Do not over-handle—this crushes pile or nap. A deep or thick pile or nap needs extra wearing ease to accommodate its bulk in the seam allowances.
Slip baste for accurate matching before stitching. Match construction to fabric type.	Test on a fabric swatch. Do not distort the plaid or stripe by steam-pressing.	Always make a muslin and work out any fitting problems in it. The less fitting, the better in this fabric, because your careful matching will have been wasted by extreme fitting. This is especially true in bias plaids.
Match border or large motifs by easing on long seams, if this is necessary.	Depends on fabric.	The ultimate is a fitting muslin; pencil on the border or placement of motifs. Fitting techniques depend on fabric. Do not fit and change placement.
Try to match ribs when stitching seams so stripes are continuous—this may be difficult. Grade and clean-finish seams.	Press lightly, as steam and a heavy hand might flatten ribs—use a press pad to protect raised ribs.	Do not grade seams or slash darts until fit is finalized. When fitting, avoid placing the points of darts on a wide or raised rib if possible.
Use small stitches and polyester thread, stretching slightly while stitching; or, use zigzag stitches. Do not stretch cut edges while basting.	Test press on a swatch; avoid steam and excessive heat. Always use a press cloth.	Allow for some give in the direction of the stretch grain. Stay shoulder seams to prevent their stretching. Always use a stretch lining or underlinings.

Progress
and
Development

At this time let us explore together the relationships and reasons for the routine of fitting, so that the insights gained might add a new dimension to your understanding *the art of fitting.* Perhaps once you have that understanding, your instincts will flourish. Now is the moment when you will actually begin to fit your fashion garment on yourself—molding and shaping to unify your style and fabric in a garment that relates to your figure exactly as intended by the designer and you.

So far we have endeavored to focus on the information which forms the background for all fitting projects. Your posture, bone structure, and weight have been evaluated, along with the right undergarments for your figure. Tools and equipment to use in a perfect setting speed you toward a sure, uncomprising fit. The tape measure has been brought into perspective, and you have formulated a trustworthy set of measurements. You should have gained insight into a pattern—the wearing ease allowed, the relationship of your figure to the total scheme, and the four basic silhouettes with variations. Style ease should no longer be a mystery, now that you understand what "Vogue's Guide To Perfect Fit of Fitted Garments" and a muslin shell can do to make your fitting successful.

Begin by absorbing some information about perfectly fitted garments. Fill in the blank areas with the details of notions, findings, accessories, and the methods used to join garment sections for a fitting. Then, put you and your garment together for the first time. From this point the pace will quicken as you relate the fabric to your needs and the style you have chosen; each dart, seam, and wrinkle will have a reason for being where it is. We will explore these reasons and help you discover them— you will see how closures, comfort, and grain influence the balance of your garment. You will also learn how to make any needed changes with expertise, and how underlining and interfacing are incorporated into fitting. After these prerequisites, fitting is developed into specifics—shoulders, back, bust, waist, hips, etc.

Points of Concern

No matter how many fashions you have successfully completed, there is always that special moment of excitement—tinged with some doubt—as you slip into your newest creation for the first time. Do you marvel at your work so far, or do you instinctively pinch in some fabric in certain areas to see what happens? Do you feel the need to tug at a neckline now that the ascot is in place? The creative seamstress who wishes to learn the finest points of fitting will benefit from the following guidelines we have formulated. These will direct her in the acquisition of the fitting skills to be used again and again throughout her ever-expanding sewing career.

Checks to Make

To approach fitting without a goal in sight is unrealistic. Here you will find a complete list of all the fitting points which are goals of primary importance.

- ☐ Garment should hang on the body and be supported by shoulders and figure contours.
- ☐ Shoulder seams should lie flat and smooth over shoulders, and extend from base of neck to shoulder bone.
- ☐ All vertical seams (including center front or back, side seams, etc.) should be perpendicular to floor.
- ☐ Waist seams (natural, dropped, or Empire) should fall on torso as indicated by illustration on pattern envelope.
- ☐ Geometric seams should lie flat and smooth with no pulling and twisting.
- ☐ Darts should lie flat and form a smooth contour, from base to point. They should point toward fullest part of the body curve they cover.
- ☐ Style details like gathers, pleats, vents, and tucks should fall smoothly.
- ☐ Pockets, trims, and other decorative details must be smooth and flat. They must also be positioned properly on the figure.
- ☐ All inner construction fabrics—underlining, interfacing, and lining—must be compatible with your fashion fabric to retain the silhouette without distortion.
- ☐ Collars and cuffs should be smooth, flat, and hug the garment.
- ☐ Jewel necklines should fit comfortably around base of neck without binding.
- ☐ Neckline variations should lie flat on the body without gaping or pulling.
- ☐ Armholes should fit smoothly around the arm whether garment has sleeves or is sleeveless.
- ☐ Sleeves should be smooth, with the needed wearing ease in both length and circumference.
- ☐ A closure should be smooth along its entire length without bulges, lumps, or distortion.
- ☐ Lapped closures should lie flat, and the fastenings should not distort the garment lines.
- ☐ Hems should hang smoothly and uniformly along the entire circumference of your garment.

Additional Pants Checks

Great-fitting pants can be yours, if you give them your all. Many of the fitting techniques to be mastered in dresses, blouses, jackets, coats, etc. are the same ones to be applied in pants and jumpsuits. However, there are a few additional check points.

- ☐ Pants should fit smoothly over your curves without exaggerating them; pants should not collapse or be strained at any point.
- ☐ The legs should fall straight to the floor without swinging off in either direction.
- ☐ The crotch should lie smoothly in front and back, and should hug the curves without restraint. The inseam should not be pulled.
- ☐ The hem of each pants leg should fall freely over the ankle bone without breaking the front leg crease at the instep.

Accessories—Seen and Unseen

A none-too-small aspect of the fitting scene are the accessories which contribute to a look and which help in determining fit. Decide what you will wear with your new fashion—from the skin out—and collect the items. Wear them for every fitting.

UNDERGARMENTS must be suited to the fashion with which they will be worn. Once selected, you must be certain to wear them for every fitting. The undergarments should fit well, causing no spare tire or thigh bulge due to an excessively tight fit. Beware of a weight gain or loss during the period of making a garment—which may be many weeks if you cannot work for long periods at a time. Panty girdles affect the fit of the crotch area of pants; if you fit them when wearing a panty girdle, plan to wear the panty girdle with the completed garment.

Check to see that your bra straps are adjusted correctly, and that your bosom is neither too low nor too high. Once you have determined the correct and most comfortable position of the apex of the bust, do not change it; doing so would affect the placement of the bust darts and perhaps ruin the fit of your garment. Refer to page 14 for more about undergarments, and remember posture (pages 12–13) can do almost as much to help your figure as can a good girdle or bra.

SHOES with heels affect the distribution of body weight by shifting your center of balance. This changes the contours of your legs and torso, and affects your manner of walking. Different heel heights will necessitate slight differences in fit and hem length. Sandals, clogs, mocassins, ghillies, saddle shoes, Mary Janes, pumps, T-straps, boots, and sneakers each suggest a function and a look that might blend with any garment you have underway. Choose a shoe that promotes the look of your garment, then coordinate the colors and textures. A shoe that is too large and heavy would ruin a feminine look, even if these shoes happen to be popular at the time. Sometimes good proportion is not in style; at such a time, you must strive for some middle ground that suits you and your needs.

HOSIERY AND JEWELRY have become more important fashion accessories now that a wide range of synthetics and plastics are available. The purpose of accessories is to add a personal and distinctive extra to a garment or an outfit. The look you are creating can be changed dramatically by brightly colored hosiery, a silk rose, or a rope of pearls. Plan ahead, even in a first fitting: the color of topstitching or buttons might be determined by that brooch you found in the attic.

BELTS AND SASHES might be worn under the bust, at the natural waistline, or at the hips. Each of these areas calls for a belt or sash that is appropriate to its placement and function. Leather belts with pewter buckles, braided soutache belts, silver chains, macramé, felt belts with enamel buckles, ribbons on suede, and patent leather belts all highlight that part of the torso where they are placed. An area that has a belt should be fitted tightly enough so that when the belt is worn, it does not hang away from body. The width and stiffness or softness of the belt will determine the placement and number of belt loops, carriers, etc. Sometimes you will have to consider using fabric rather than thread belt loops at side seams, because the stress on the loops will be great. This is more likely to occur in wrap-style garments whose fit is dependent on the belt or sash. Test belt loop length beforehand.

NECKWEAR—a scarf, dickey, or ascot—that will complete an outfit has bearing on the fit and shape of your neckline. A neckline that otherwise appears too low or too loose will be perfect, once the scarf has been slipped into place. A scarf tied into a cowboy bib or pussy-cat bow will add a distinctive touch to an otherwise simple fashion. A little turtleneck dickey is the answer for the woman who wants to wear a layered look, but who is a bit too full-figured to do so. A wide silk tie supports, fills out, and adds polish to a shirt and vest look. These diverse neckwear accessories add color, texture, and individuality to your garment. It is up to you to plan ahead and strive for the fit that will accommodate your accessory whims.

SWEATERS became chic in the thirties, and they have not lost their fashion power yet. Ribbed tweeds, silk jerseys, openwork raschel knits, skinny-ribbed knit undershirts, and shrugs of bouclé or novelty yarns are just some of the sweater looks available to you in planning an outfit. This may be as modest as a jumper or pinafore worn over a sweater, but its fit will be directly related to the fit of the sweater underneath. Early in the fitting game, you must decide what your sweater plan is, so that you can build a garment that will show off you and your sweater to a "T." Refer to fitting layered garments (page 77) for more information.

Shape Insurance For Your New-born Creation

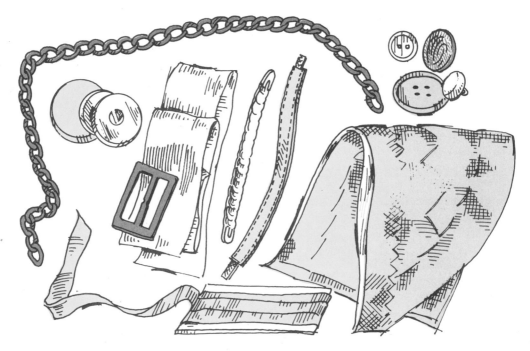

How rewarding it is to create a garment that fits you and makes you look great! You will exude confidence and poise as you stride down the street in an outfit that is totally smashing. You wear your garment again and again because it makes you feel marvelous—but then something begins to happen. Much too soon your creation starts looking dog-eared. The neckline seems to stretch, the hemline dips a bit, the puffy sleeve collapses, and the buttons pull and distort the front of the garment. In horror, you wonder what happened, as your new-born star slips into oblivion.

Notions and findings are the unsung heroes of clothes that fit and will continue to do so. Tape stitched into the seam supports bias, shaped, or straight seams; shoulder pads support well-mounted sleeves; stays and belting hold areas rigid; hooks, snaps, and buttons fasten edges; and interfacing, underlining, and linings insure a long, hardy life for your garment. Interfacing is placed in garment areas that will be under stress, that are bias, or that have corners, scallops, or points which require special support to guarantee that the shape will not be distorted. Underlining is used to stabilize a garment and to act as a support for inner construction. Linings not only add to the durability of your garment, but they polish your garment's interior too.

The creative woman who sews is a bit of a sculptress, for she is molding two-dimensional fabric into a three-dimensional form. That form must be permanently built in to withstand the wear and tear of daily use and normal care. To shortchange your garment in terms of inner construction is to plot its early demise. Using the proper notions and findings when they are needed is your best shape insurance.

TAPES: There are several choices to be made to find the tape that will do its job perfectly. Use ribbon seam binding for straight seams or edges to prevent stretch and to form a restrictive edge. Stretched commercial single-fold bias tape is used for curved edges, contour seams, or straight edges where seam binding may cause puckering. To prepare it, press open folds and stretch as you press to remove slack. Cut strip in half lengthwise. Shape to match garment curves. Use pre-shrunk ribbon seam binding or cotton twill tape for jackets and coats when tailoring.

SHOULDER PADS: These are used in coats, jackets, and dresses where the shoulder line is accented and slightly elevated. Sometimes, shoulder pads can be used to correct sloping or narrow shoulders, or to give lift to the sleeve styling—as in puff sleeves, T-seamed sleeves, shoulder lines with epaulettes, or shoulder extensions. They are available in dress and coat weights in a variety of shapes, and are fabric-covered or plain. Select washable shoulder pads for use in washable garments.

STAYS: These metal or plastic spirals are used for shaping, molding, and for vertical reinforcement. They come in 4″, 6″, or 8″ lengths. Boning is often used for similar purposes. Short plastic stays support the points of shirt collars.

WEIGHTS: To help control the drape and fall of the garment, lead weights can be effectively used. These range in size from ¼″ to 1⅛″, and can be encased in fabric before they are applied to the garment. Strips of lead pellets encased in fabric are sold by the yard, and chain weights can be purchased in different weights and widths. These types are usually sewn along hem allowances. The fall of a cowl neckline or a jacket front can also be controlled by weights.

BELTING: A sturdy but flexible shaper, belting is used for custom made belts. It comes in widths ranging from ½″ to 3″, and is available in black or white. There are regular and iron-on types which come pre-packaged or which can be purchased by the yard. Making your own professional-looking belt is as important as any other factor in the success of your garment. Always take the time and care to choose the correct belt width and the perfect buckle or clasp, because these can add even more fashion to your garment than was originally built into it.

BUTTONS: Plastic, metal, wood, leather, or bone buttons can serve two functions at the same time—they fasten the garment and decorate it. When the garment is closed properly by buttons, it will be balanced vertically and horizontally. The buttons should be chosen in proportion to the garment and your figure. Buttons should be placed at areas of stress—bust, waist, and hips—and remaining buttons should be evenly spaced between these. When an ornate or ball button interferes with a belt at the waistline, replace it with one that is flat and will not cause a bulge. Or, you can substitute a hook and eye or a snap for this button. When a button is placed on a shirt or jacket, the button should be carefully placed to control the roll of the lapel and collar without distorting it. If the garment is gaping between buttons, sometimes it is necessary to add snaps to correct this.

Making Connections

Either of two methods can be used to join your garment sections together for the first fitting: basting or pinning. Each method has its advantages, and your skills will determine which is best for your fabric and you. Once the structural pieces of the garment are either basted or pinned together, the garment will be ready for a fitting where further pinning and marking is made on the figure.

Basted Fittings

When basting your garment together for a fitting, use thread in a contrasting color, and backstitch every 3″–6″. Silk thread is preferable, because it will not leave marks when pressed. When you are further along in the construction of collars and facings, it will be especially important that no impressions from thread basting remain on the outside of your garment.

Generally your garment is basted right sides together, using *even basting*. The seam allowances are finger-pressed open; for firm, crisp fabrics you may need a little steam, as well, but never rest the iron on the fabric and form creases. If you are using a fabric whose design must be matched, use *slip basting*. When working on metallics or beaded garments, it is recommended that you lap the edges, matching seamlines; baste, using even or *diagonal basting* to support the fabric. Make your thread tracings with *uneven basting*.

To baste *stretchable fabrics* like knits, crepes, or those cut on the bias, make even, loose stitches with a doubled thread. Secure thread at top of seam

and work down; backstitch at end, leaving 12″ of thread hanging. Use as many lengths of thread as necessary to complete the seam. When trying on the garment, distribute fabric along basting threads and adjust as needed. **Machine basting** may be used for firm fabrics that are not easily marred or when only a minimum of fitting is anticipated, as it may leave permanent marks. It should be done by the woman who is secure and certain about her ability at the machine and the durability of the fabric with which she will be working.

When you decide which basting method is appropriate for your fashion and fabric, baste darts, but do not machine stitch them until after trying on the garment. Then place the garment pieces together, matching notches, centers, and darts; join the pieces, pinning, then basting along the seamline.

Pin Fittings

A pin fitting refers to joining the garment sections together with pins, and then trying on the garment. When pinning the sections together, have the fabric right side out and pin with the seam allowances *wrong sides* together. Use sharp, silk dressmaker pins that are clean, straight, and rust-free; a bent pin will cause little bumps which distort the smooth pin line for which you are striving. For certain knits, you may need ball point pins. Follow the procedure for basting, matching darts, centers, notches, etc.

The pins should be placed parallel to the cut edge on the seamline; usually, pinning every 2″–3″ will suffice. In curved areas, pin every 1″–2″. Catch only a small amount of fabric on each pin; adjust this amount according to the thickness of the fabric. The seamlines should lie smooth and flat. For a set-in sleeve, place pins horizontally.

Pin basting should not be used for hard-surfaced fabrics like vinyl or satin. On slippery, silky fabrics, use pins sparingly. The best method for you may be a combination: pin basting for major seams and some darts, and thread basting for garment areas that are more intricate or require greater control and stability. Refer to pages 36–41 for information on fitting particular fabric types.

Your Fabric Takes Form

Because the *major* pattern changes you made to compensate for figure flaws, posture, or variance from standard measurement do not alone ensure custom fit in your particular fashion fabric, it will be necessary to make further *minor* changes during fitting. We must stress that these are truly minor changes—amounting to no more than a fraction of an inch—but that they have been exaggerated when illustrated in order for you to see them.

Fitting now involves trying on your fashion and marking changes, removing it and pinning or basting the changes, and finally trying it on again for a check before stitching. In most cases, you will be able to do the fitting yourself, but if someone else can fit you, the task will be easier. If you do not have a fitter and your fashion has a back closure, baste a zipper in place so that you can try on the garment for the fitting. To cut wider seam allowances, see pages 58–59.

A Status Report

A quick review is in order—put on the proper undergarments and have all accessories, notions, and tools handy. Baste underlining, if used, to each fashion fabric piece; pin or baste interfacing in place (page 59). Vertical centers and folds and crosswise grain indications should be thread traced on each garment piece. Staystitch neck and armhole curves. Baste darts, and add ease and gathering stitches. (Make them by hand if machine stitching would permanently damage your fashion fabric.) Join only those garment sections representing the *shell*. Collars, facings, sleeves, cuffs, pockets, etc. will be fitted later.

Now for the first time you will see how well your design and fabric are working together. Concentrate on the fabric as you ease it into the correct position and smooth out any wrinkles. Expect high necklines and snug armholes, since the seam allowances have not yet been turned in the proper direction. *Do not clip* until you have read page 54. Should you find a wrinkle or a pulled seam, review pages 56–58.

On the following pages each garment area as well as stylized features will be defined and specific fitting adjustments indicated. The particular needs for classic garments are emphasized as you assemble the shell for a fitting. Read the section on layered garments (page 77) if your sewing project includes garments worn over one another. To secure closures properly, see pages 52–53.

DRESSES: An infinite number of designs are derived from the four basic silhouettes (page 26) which can be manipulated endlessly by creative designers. With your clearer understanding of wearing and style ease, you will know not to over-fit the shell, as this would make your dress unattractive or ruin its style lines.

BLOUSES: Generally, blouses and shirt shells are fitted just as you would a dress. The special factor to consider at this point is the other garment—skirt, pants, or jumper—and how it will affect the fit. Blouse style variations demand further refinements of fit to complement your figure.

SKIRTS: Pin hem along proposed hemline. When fitting, strive for a smooth fit over the hips, and a comfortably snug fit at the waistline. Do not fit the waist too tightly, however, as the waistband or facing may take up some of the wearing ease allowed. Baste either twill tape or ribbon seam binding along the seamline so skirt will not stretch as you evaluate it and the other garment with which it will be worn. Remember that a blouse that is worn tucked into the skirt may affect its fit.

JACKETS AND COATS: Consider your jacket shell first, as the same layers of clothes must be in place to fit it as to fit a coat. Your jacket pattern has ease built into it so that it can be worn over a dress or blouse; coats have enough built-in ease to fit over a jacket. However, when the jacket is a cut-off version of a coat design, the two cannot be worn one over the other, as ease does not exist for this. Also, be wary of your *interpretation* of a design: the top of a two-piece dress may look like a jacket to you, but it will not fit like one. Since outer garments usually demand more fabric layers, expect underlining, interfacing, interlining, and lining to play a crucial role in fit. Baste all layers together along centers for stability. Take into consideration the type of lining you will be using— for light- to medium weight linings, see pages 87–88; for bulky linings, page 78. If your project is a tailored jacket, see The Vogue Sewing Book, pages 336–358.

PANTS: Fitting should be minimal since you took the time to build your personal needs into the pattern before cutting. Shoes and heel height are interrelated with the hem length. Pin the hem to a proposed length. Focus on fit at waist, hip, thigh, crotch and leg, as well as your choice of tops. See pages 68–69. To complete the hem, turn to page 91.

Closures

Getting in and out of your garment is dependent on the type, size, and placement of your closure. This can be located at center front or center back, a side seam, or it can take the form of double-breasted or asymmetrical styling. Closures in shoulder seams or in raglan sleeve style lines are functional, too. When fitting, use the center front and center back of your garment as a guide in establishing its balance and fit, regardless of the type or location of closure. You must pin closures properly to keep the garment balanced and free from distortion.

ZIPPERS: To fit a garment that will have a zipper, pin closure smoothly and securely. Turn in one edge along the closure seamline and pin; then match the folded edge to the seamline of the opposite edge. Pin the two edges together; place pins perpendicular to seamline for a smooth fit. Use enough pins so closure area will not come apart during the fitting. If a back zipper, someone will have to pin it for you.

LAPPED EDGES: Closures that lap can be found at center front or back, in double-breasted or asymmetrical closings, and at shoulders. The overlap prevents gaping. When fitting, place pins at areas of stress—bust, waist, and hips. Additional pins will keep the garment closed and in place during fitting.

The center or placement markings should have been thread traced. Match these markings when pinning the closure. Check to see that the lengthwise grain on each half of the garment is straight along the centers. If your garment requires interfacing, baste it in position (see page 59). When fitting, the centers should remain in position at all times. Shifting them to let out or take in a garment will distort both balance and neckline fit. Pin an extended facing in its finished position. When fitting double-breasted garments, use enough pins to support the weight of the garment, overlap, and inner edges of underlap.

ASYMMETRICAL EDGES: This is a closure placed other than at a garment center, falling at any angle to the left or right of it. An asymmetrical closing can be short or the length of the garment. Some asymmetrically wrapped garments are similar to double-breasted garments; each side of the garment is cut symmetrically, but the way it is fastened will make the garment appear asymmetrical. In a wrap garment, the overlap is large so the garment will not separate as you move. The overlap is often cut at an angle, and the resulting bias edge is very stretchy; take care not to over-handle or stretch it. First pin the garment together along the matched center fronts, placing the pins perpendicular to the marking. If necessary, support the underlap and overlap edges with pins to prevent design distortion.

For asymmetrical garments in which each side of the garment is cut differently, pin fronts together matching centers; place pins vertically along overlapping edge. Some garments have an asymmetrical band insert which depends on slashing the front section of garment. Pin or baste the seams together, leaving one side front seam open; if the garment has a jewel neckline, leave part of a shoulder seam open. Slip into the garment without slashing the band opening, and close seams with pins. After fitting the body of the garment, continue band construction.

MEETING EDGES: Garment edges which meet at the center and do not overlap ultimately will be secured by loops and buttons, buckles, or laces, or hang unfastened. These edges may have an applied or extended facing.

When fitting a closure with meeting edges, baste any interfacing in place. For an applied facing, pin the edges together along center front; match seamline and place pins vertically. Pin an extended facing as for a lapped closure. To fit, baste one folded edge to seam binding or twill tape; pin the remaining edge to it, with folds meeting. This closure must not gape or pull open. Leave ease to accommodate garments worn underneath.

KNITS: When fitting closures in stable knits, no special procedures are needed other than those discussed for the various closings. For moderate stretch or stretchable unbonded knits, support closure edges with tape if they will not be interfaced. If the closure edges are shaped or cut at an angle, be certain that you handle them gently to avoid distortion or stretching.

53

Comfort in a Fashion Fabric Shell

There are two important things to consider after you have joined together your garment shell and are trying it on for the first time. These considerations are the restriction caused by the unfinished seam allowance and the reactions of your body movements with your fabric. Fitting is most crucial if the garment binds at neck and armholes, or if you find that the garment is a little snug. Wear a belt if the garment calls for one—or tie a piece of ribbon seam binding around your body at the spot where you plan to wear your belt.

TO RELEASE SEAM ALLOWANCES during a fitting is sometimes necessary, but it must be done with extreme care. To clip indiscriminately may cause trouble when you are sewing the garment together. Clip a seam allowance only at the point of strain, and avoid clipping into the seamline. If you find one clip does not relieve the strain, make a few additional clips at even intervals on each side of the first. Clips made thoughtlessly prohibit exact fit if you find that a seamline needs to be raised or let out slightly.

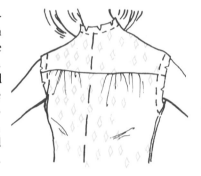

TEST FOR COMFORT before you actually fit. Sit and stoop in various positions. Move your arms, testing the stresses to which you will subject this particular garment; make sure the armhole opening in the shell is adequate for a set-in sleeve, and re-check this with the sleeve basted in place. Raglan and kimono sleeves, too, should have the proper ease for livability. Walk at your normal pace; go up some stairs if it is a fitted garment. Evaluate bust, waist, and hip fit. The garment should be smooth and unrestraining. Remember that a fitted garment can never offer the freedom of movement that is found in a loosely fitted garment. To resolve specific problem areas in the current stage of fitting, turn to the related sections in this chapter.

Grain Perfection

When something is irritating or contrary to one's nature, it is colloquially described as "going against the grain." Many people are not aware that wood, leather, and stone all have grain, and that the term refers to the arrangement of component fibers, layers, or particles. In fabric, the grain describes the position of yarns, and when this is not handled with respect to its inherent characteristics — if you go against the grain — the garment will hang askew. Straight grain hangs straight, and there is nothing you can do to change it. If the straight grain is distorted by a seam, the twisting that results is caused by the grain not falling perpendicular to the floor.

Most garments are cut on the lengthwise grain for a more stable and durable garment. When not cut on a straight grain, a garment will tend to hang with the grain anyway. The part of the garment that has been cut slightly off-grain will twist and sag until the grain can fall in a plumb line directly perpendicular to the floor.

To check the grain of your garment, use a plumb line (see page 18); with experience you may be able to see the fabric grain without one. As an aid, thread trace the center front, center back (if not a seam), the lengthwise center of each sleeve, and the crosswise grains. For pants, thread trace lengthwise grain at crease line or center front and back of each leg. Thread trace crosswise grain at the hip area. If legs are full below knee, they may not be on straight grain at the centers.

When fitting, look for grain distortions indicated by twisting, sagging, or wrinkling. Any vertical seams or lengthwise thread tracings should parallel the plumb line in a true perpendicular to the floor. Crosswise thread tracings should be at right angles to the vertical indications. Style ease variations in the garment are an area to consider. In skirts — like A-line and gored — the seams will be shaped at an angle; these fall on a partial bias angle (not true bias). The grain chevrons at the shaped seam, yet must balance to avoid wrinkles and twisting. The grain of a full circular skirt goes from right angles to bias and back to right angles.

If a grainline is hanging slightly askew, it can often be smoothed out and corrected by opening a nearby seam and smoothing it into position (see pages 56–57 for the technique). If the fabric wrinkles and pulls, causing much grain distortion, you must check further. In Book III you will find the alterations in a fitting muslin that will be needed to correct problems and make the garment conform to your contours. Your figure, with its individual shape, will affect the hang of the grain; alterations will compensate for your particular contours by allowing enough fabric to reposition the grain so it falls straight. Your job in fitting is to further refine the alignment of lengthwise and crosswise grains of your fabric.

Simple Compensations

Regardless of your method for assembling your garment shell for a fitting, it will be easy to make minor compensations to achieve perfect fit. Begin to fit your garment at the shoulders and work down to the hem; for pants, work from the waist to the hem. In each area apply the fitting techniques found on pages 59–95.

You now have the opportunity to explore the drape and fit of your garment on you. When you have determined those areas which need fitting, you have the option of re-pinning the garment on you, or making the changes with chalk while wearing the garment. In either case, you then remove and re-baste or re-pin the garment on your dress form; or, you may have someone make the changes on you (even slip-stitching them securely). Sometimes you must use a combination of techniques.

When fitting, remember that garment sections are interrelated. You can understand and predict these relationships if you use your head and let your fitting instincts guide you. There are times when you may have to take in a garment, making both seam allowances wider, or let out a garment, making both seam allowances narrower. *Do not* let out a seam more than 3/8″ — you will need at least a 1/4″ wide seam allowance for stability. For ravelly or delicate fabrics, stitch seam binding or lace to the narrowed seam allowance. If you are working with a zipper opening in very heavy fabric, you may need to extend the seam allowance with a 1″ bias strip of light-weight fabric in order to later insert the zipper.

Most times you will not change an entire seam; taper the change gradually into the original seamline. Be aware that both seam allowances will not necessarily be changed equal amounts; always retain one point on the seam to match a point on another garment section circumference (such as a shoulder seam correction where the sleeve or facing to be applied will still need the same circumference) or seams (such as a bodice joining skirt or pants unit). Make circumference adjustments of 1″ or less at the side seams; otherwise, divide the changes by the number of seams (other than a center front or center back seam) and make equal changes on each seam.

If you have purchased a stripe, plaid, or luxury fabric, refer to pages 57–58. For stretchable unbonded knits, plan wider seam allowances (pages 58–59).

BASTED FITTING CHANGES: There are a number of ways to baste your garment together for a fitting. Think first of seams that are not interrupted by

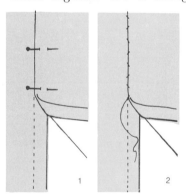

darts, etc. — the procedure is quite simple. You can pin or baste the changes into position while on the figure; you can mark them with pins or chalk; or, you can pin out excess fabric along seams and make changes after the garment has been removed. Let your fabric determine the method you use.

To pin the changes while on the figure, remove the basting. Turn in one edge the amount of change and lap it over other edge; match fold to the new or old seamline. Pin at right angles to the fold to hold layers together (1), or slip baste the fold in place (2).

For darts, release basting from seam and dart; re-shape or re-position (pages 59–60) by pinning the two layers together, shaping the dart along proposed stitching lines (1). Remove the garment, turn it wrong side out, and mark the fabric along pins with chalk. Be sure to allow for the inside bulk of the dart. To slip baste dart, crease it along one new stitching line and sew the fold in place along the other (2).

NEW SEAMLINE

To mark needed changes with chalk or pins, first test which method is right for your fabric. After fitting, thread trace chalk marks. *Never* use pens or lead pencils to mark your fashion fabric (although permanent marks are quite desirable and useful on your fitting muslin). This method is used for marking new seamlines at neck and armholes, or placement lines for pockets, trims, etc.

PIN FITTING CHANGES: While this method permits quicker changes, it presents a few problems. *Fabric bulk* demands first consideration—when bulky extended seam allowances and darts have been turned to the inside of the garment, they consume vital wearing ease. As you fit, adjust the seams as needed, pinning carefully along the new seamlines; remember to allow for the inside bulk the seam allowances will eventually create. Pin darts carefully along the new stitching lines. Place pins close together in a smooth line. Transfer changes to the wrong side of the fabric.

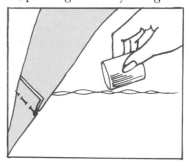

To mark new neck and armhole seamlines and placement lines, use pins with plastic heads or mark with chalk, testing first. After making all fitting changes, remove garment and mark each side of the seam or dart before removing pins.

FITTING SPECIAL FABRICS: Although we discussed the general fitting problems inherent in fabrics on pages 32–35, and then emphasized the techniques with charts on pages 36–41, there are some special situations to be considered when making fitting changes. Luxurious or unusual fabrics represent a considerable investment on your part so if you are working with a silhouette for the first time, make the garment in muslin which has a similar hand to resolve your fitting problems. Machine baste the muslin together; on the inside, take a pen and mark the stitching line on each side of seams and darts permanently. Mark a lengthwise fabric thread for a grainline. Rip the muslin garment apart and press it flat. Use this for your pattern, placing the wrong side of the muslin on the wrong side of the folded fashion fabric.

Plaids (even or uneven), *stripes* (balanced or unbalanced, and vertical or horizontal), *design motifs,* and *border prints* must be strategically placed when laying out the pattern pieces. They must match at pattern seamlines before cutting out your fabric. Because of this, you must have an accurately adjusted pattern; you *cannot make major fitting changes* in either length or circumference without destroying your careful preplanned matching. *Glamorous fabrics* with metallic threads, beads, or surface interest should have a test muslin, also.

Knitted fabrics have the very desirable characteristic of recovery that allows them to stretch while being worn and then return to their original shape when removed. Scientific innovations have created very stable, resilient fibers that increase the recovery of knits. To achieve great fit, you will need to know a little more about the variables you may find in the knitted fabric you have purchased. *Stable* knits have a limited degree of stretch or give, and are used in their relaxed state. When fitting, handle them like their woven counterparts; these knits move with the body and absorb the strain of wear—the garment will return to its original shape without split seams, etc.

Some knits have *moderate stretch* characteristics which are neither stable or stretchable. You may need some help to arrive at a well-fitting garment. When fitting, stay areas that need stabilizing (shoulder seams, opening edges, etc.) by basting stretched bias tape in place on one edge of the seam; it can later be stitched permanently. These knits can provide a slinky, clinging fit over body contours. Be sure that the silhouette calls for a close fit in these areas, or you will ruin the shape.

Stretchable knits are meant for body-revealing styles and must be fitted with this in mind. Check your pattern circumference (pages 28–30) before cutting your fabric. For more fit insurance, cut wider seam allowances (see below). Stay areas that need to be stabilized during fitting as for moderate stretch knits.

WIDER SEAM ALLOWANCES may help turn your fashion fabric into a beautifully fitted garment. Heavy, thick, firm, and textured woven or knitted fabrics will often need wider seam allowances simply because more of them is taken up in turning and pressing open or enclosing raw edges than would be for a fabric of lesser substance. When you work with fabrics unknown to you, give yourself the fitting insurance you need. Make the *vertical seam allowances* 1″–1½″ wide when cutting out your fabric so you will have that extra pinch that might be needed to mold the fabric to your body.

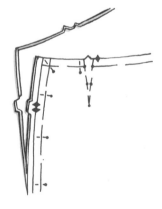

Pants must be considered specifically—you may already have had the experience of making a style in a woven and then in a knit, only to find the woven a little snug for livability and the crotch a bit too low in the knit. Here is where wider seam allowances would have been your answer. Fabrics often do strange things to the crotch and inseams of pants, so special consideration should be made before cutting them out. This is especially important in moderately stretchy or stretchable knits, loosely woven or soft fabrics, and bias-cut designs. Simply make the seam allowance 2½″–3″ wide at the lower crotch curve on both front and back. Continue cutting in a smooth line up the inseam cutting line to the width desired; cut across to the crotch seam cutting line, tapering in a smooth curve to notches.

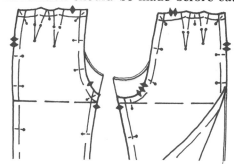

Fitting With Under Fabrics

Fitting a garment with *underlining* requires a keen eye—look for imprints of bubbles or ridges in the underlining that interfere with the smoothness of your fashion fabric. If this occurs, release the seams, darts, or opening edges, and working with the grain, eliminate the underlining problems. Underlining may also interfere with the hang of the garment if both grains have not been aligned correctly; wrinkles or pulling may appear along a seam. Correct this as you would any grain distortion. For the handling of underlining, see The Vogue Sewing Book, pages 184 and 384.

To fit a garment with *interfacing,* this must first be basted in place along the seamlines or secure it with pins if your fabric will not mar. For openings, baste the interfacing to the garment shell along the center markings; for extended facings, turn them to the outside along the foldline, and pin or baste along the neckline. Try on your garment shell—the interfacing should mold smoothly with the fashion fabric. If bubbles or ridges occur in the shell or the interfacing, remove the pins and, working with the grain, smooth the garment over the interfacing; pin the interfacing as it falls. Make sure lapels roll smoothly by turning them to the outside along the proposed roll; re-pin interfacing if necessary. When the interfacing relates perfectly to your body contours and the garment shell, secure it and continue fitting.

Fitting Darts

Fabric weight and drape affect the fit of darts built into your garment to accommodate body contours. The placement and depth of the darts control how the fabric will flow around your curves. Before changing a bust dart, adjust bra straps to the position that is most attractive and provides a youthful uplift. Bust darts should end ½″–1″ from the apex of the bust. When re-pinning or re-basting each dart, be certain that it lies smoothly and unpuckered, and tapers to a point; see page 56 for methods to make fitting changes. In medium to heavyweight fabrics, a small dart will not lie flat; in this stage of fitting, do not be concerned.

Any dart should point toward the fullest part of a body contour—bust, hip, shoulder blade, etc. Depending on fabric weight, you may need to change the length or depth of the dart, or shift it slightly to avoid distorting fabric design. Try to balance darts on the right and left sides of your garment even when you have asymmetrical figure flaws. Book III covers the specific shaping for each figure flaw.

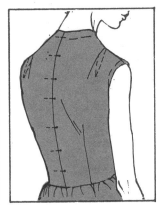

Darts in *knits* may require a little more consideration. Because knitted fabrics have a tendency to cling, care must be taken to reduce the bulk of fabric layers and any ridges caused by undergarments. When darts are made in knits, they cling even closer to the body. When fitting darts in knit fabric, place pins close together, as knits are stretchy and the pins might fall out. Basting darts may be more appropriate.

Darts in *skirts, pants,* or skirt portions of a *cut-in-one* bodice and skirt are significant in that the waist and hip are crucial fitting areas. Special figure contours will affect the depth and placement of the darts (see pages 66–69). Baste these darts securely, since they will be subjected to much stress during fitting.

Shoulders

On your shoulders rests the balance and weight of the entire garment; it is essential that your shoulder area fits properly. The seam of a regular shoulder line should rest on top of the shoulder and extend from the base of the neck to the arm hinge. The fit of an extended or dropped shoulder line depends on the styling of a specific design; the shoulder line will extend beyond the edge of the shoulder bone. When the shoulder seam has been adjusted to your personal contours, the fit of the armhole and sleeve may be affected. Raglan and kimono sleeve styles involve specific fitting techniques (see pages 64–65).

It is customary to begin fitting in the shoulder area, for any minor corrections made here will affect the fit and balance of the entire garment. For any shoulder changes, take into account fabric weight and wearing ease. The shoulder and armhole areas must have enough ease comfort for motion.

To increase girth for *broad shoulders,* re-mark the armhole seamline. Because you did not clip into your armhole haphazardly, there is fabric for this. To decrease girth for *narrow shoulders,* re-mark seamline, taking a larger seam allowance.

To further adjust the angle for *sloping shoulders,* pin in excess fabric along shoulder, tapering to neck seamline. Drop the lower armhole seamline the same amount; re-mark. If your garment will accommodate shoulder pads, these may correct sloping shoulders. To give yourself more armhole circumference for *square shoulders,* let out shoulder seam at edge of armhole, tapering to neck seamline. Raise armhole seamline at underarm the same amount; remark.

 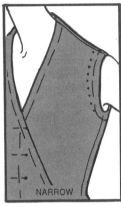 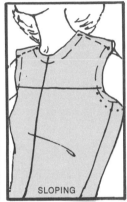 

If you have made a shoulder adjustment, each back shoulder dart, if any, should be moved to the center of the new shoulder line and point to the shoulder blade. Re-shape dart to fit. This applies to darts, pleats, or tucks in the bodice front; adjust spacing and length as needed (see pages 73–75 as a guide).

Back

Your garment should fit smoothly and be wrinkle-free across the back. If you find when fitting your fashion garment that there are horizontal or vertical wrinkles in the back, these can be corrected by changing the length or circumference of the bodice back, by remarking seamlines, or by adjusting darts.

You may find that the *center back seam* of your garment is in need of some small adjustment. If a soft, stretchy fabric will not drape smoothly across the back and causes wrinkles, take in the center back seam a minimal amount. If your fabric is crisp, and medium to heavy in weight, let out the center back seam a minimal amount for more ease. For a narrow back, see page 164. Note: When you adjust the back, the grain may chevron rather than balance; this is quite acceptable, but may be pronounced in stripes or plaids.

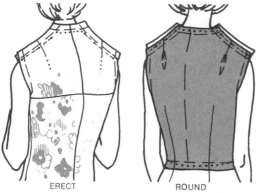

ERECT   ROUND

If bodice back wrinkles above shoulder blades, it may be due to a ***very erect back.*** When fitting, pin out excess fabric at neck and shoulder, and re-shape darts to fit. The back neck and shoulder seam allowances will become larger, tapering to original width at armhole. If you have a ***rounded back,*** bodice back will pull up at shoulders and waist. When fitting, let out back shoulder and neck edges (seam allowances will become narrower), tapering to original width at armhole. Re-shape darts to fit. For additional length, let out waist seam across center of back, tapering to original width at sides.

The Bust Area

When fitting your fashion fabric in the bust area, you may be dealing with darts, geometric or contour seaming, or no darts at all. It is the draping of these styled areas over your body contours which determines any minor fitting changes to be made in your fashion fabric. The weight and drape of your fabric and their effect on the wearing ease will influence minor changes in bust fit.

DARTS: The underarm and front bust darts may need small changes if you find wrinkling and fullness across the bust. To decrease cupping, make darts narrower, tapering toward apex in a smooth point; take out an additional amount at the side and waist seam allowances of the bodice front. You may have to re-shape the armhole seamline. Your garment may pull over the bust, and the waist may pull at sides. To increase cupping, make darts

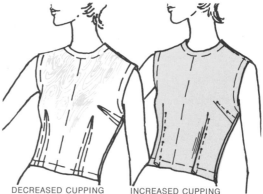

DECREASED CUPPING INCREASED CUPPING

deeper, tapering toward apex in a smooth point. Let out side and waist seam allowances, and open your sleeve seams at armhole the same amount.

GEOMETRIC SEAMING: There are many geometric seaming details that incorporate bust fit. When fitting garments of this type, do not fit too tightly over body contours, as this distorts the fabric. The difficulty in fitting garments with curved or angular seaming is adjusting the shaped seaming without destroying the balance and proportion. In garments whose design is dependent on the proportion and balance of decorative seaming, any change in seams to adjust the fit may affect the fashion impact. Make small fitting changes in the shoulder or side seams where they will be least obvious; keep other seam changes to a minimum.

PRINCESS SEAMING: The bust area should fit smoothly over the apex of the bust. If you find the fullest part of the bustline shaping too high or too low due to the drape of your fashion fabric, re-shape the bustline seaming, tapering smoothly to the original seamlines. For a princess line that is too tight, release and let out seams over the bust, tapering to the original seamline above and below. For a princess-line that is too loose, take in the seam allowances over the bust area, retaining the style line.

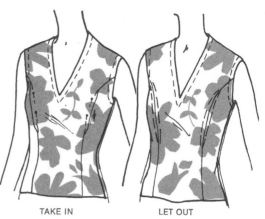

TAKE IN   LET OUT

NO DARTS: Never fit too tightly. Since fit is dependent on fabric drape, do not pull the fabric out of alignment in either full or body-hugging designs.

TO ELIMINATE A BUST DART: Knit and bias-cut garments are naturals for fitting without darts, but other fabrics can also be fitted to accommodate the no-bra look. Remove basting from bust darts and underarm seams. Add an ease thread in dart area along underarm seam edge. Fit garment over bust, working out any excess fabric in armhole. Re-mark armhole seamline.

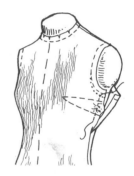

Necklines

The style referred to as the jewel neckline is the point from which all other necklines evolve. A styled neckline will vary from this basic neck-hugging fit according to how much higher or lower it is from the base of the back neck; Vogue Patterns has indicated on back pattern pieces the extent of this variation at the center back. However, in some styles the back neckline will remain at the base of the back neck, but the front neckline will drop; in other styles, both the front and back may be lowered.

JEWEL: You may have to raise or lower your neckline. For a medium to heavyweight fabric, lower neck seamline; collars and facings will also add bulk. Make a slightly wider seam allowance when finishing neckline. Or, raise the seamline, using a narrow seam allowance.

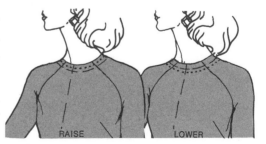

RAISE   LOWER

GAPING: Low necklines like V- or U-shapes may gape in your fashion fabric. Adjust by lifting bodice front at shoulder near neck to remove excess fabric between bust apex and shoulder. Taper adjustment to armhole so shoulder lies flat.

DÉCOLLETÉ OR LOW-CUT: Refer to page 144 to test before cutting your fashion fabric. If, after you have cut your fashion garment, the neckline is still too low, try to pick up a bit of fabric in the shoulder seams as suggested for gaping necklines; or, use a narrow neck seam allowance.

KNITS: When fitting the neckline of a stable knit, handle your fabric gently. Other knits are very stretchy and should not be over-handled, pulled, or strained. If you are not using interfacing, baste tape before fitting the neckline of a stretchy knit.

The Armhole Area

An evaluation of armhole fit in your fashion fabric is in order as you proceed with fitting. Not only may this involve the standard armhole, but also the design features of raglan and kimono sleeves (with or without gussets). This area is vital to comfortable fit, so approach each garment realistically—a jacket armhole should not fit like a dress. Fit a jacket (or coat) over the garment you intend wearing under it, as the circumference must be large enough to accommodate the other garment.

STANDARD ARMHOLES: This area may have been resolved by previous adjustments. If you have had no other fitting problem, test the armhole now—the underarm seamline should be about 1″ below the armpit. If too tight, let out the shoulder and underarm seams, tapering to original width; if too loose, take in shoulder and underarm seams, tapering to original width. Re-shape underarm area of armhole if needed. Make the same changes in sleeve underarm or facing seamlines.

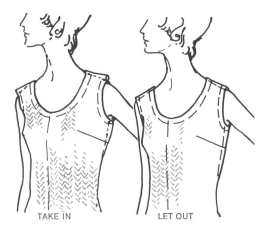

TAKE IN   LET OUT

RAGLAN SLEEVES: Baste shoulder darts or seams and underarm seams; then baste both sleeves into garment. Test sleeves with arm relaxed and in motion. The sharpest curve of the shoulder dart or seam should fall over the shoulder hinge. Re-shape dart or seam to fit this contour, using the standard shoulder seam fitting adjustments (pages 60–61) as a guide, Underarm seam should fall about 1″ below armpit and arm movement should be free without pulling or straining. Remove basting across underarm between notches and raise or lower the underarm curve as needed, taking a deeper or narrower seam allowance on bodice while maintaining sleeve seam allowance, fit back and neck at seam so the garment lies smoothly over these areas. Remember that fit of raglan sleeves at neck edge must be considered as well.

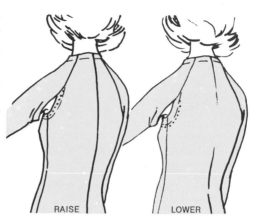

RAISE　　　LOWER

KIMONO SLEEVES: High fit with a gusset, dolman, or batwing sleeve are variations of this sleeve. When these sleeves are very wide, they are more restrictive than when narrow. The garment is involved, so do not over-fit. The sharpest curve of the shoulder seam should fall over the shoulder hinge. Re-shape shoulder seams to fit, if needed; use the standard shoulder seam fitting adjustments (refer to pages 60–62) as a guide.

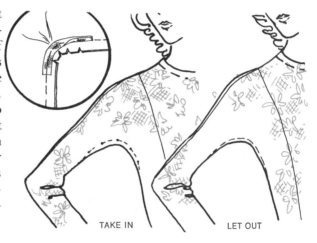

TAKE IN　　　LET OUT

For kimono sleeves *without gussets,* center a strip of bias tape (stretched and shaped to match the curve) over the underarm curve as you baste the seam for a fitting. Clip this curve, but do so with discretion—no more than ¼″ until you test the fit. Fit shoulder seams first. Then, take in or let out the underarm area if needed.

For kimono sleeves *with gussets,* reinforce points along the stitching lines, and baste any darts or seams in the gusset. Slash garment to within ¼″ of point between stitching lines. From the outside, position garment over gusset; baste, matching stitching lines to gusset seamlines. Keep reinforcement patches on outside. Fit shoulder seams first, then gusset and garment, taking in and letting out underarm area as needed. (Remember to consider uncompleted slashing.) Mark adjustments on gusset.

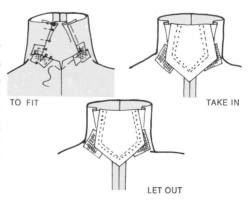

TO FIT　　　TAKE IN

LET OUT

KNITS: When fitting armholes, and raglan and kimono sleeves in a knitted fabric, follow the previously stated procedures. If you found it necessary to support shoulders and necklines with tape to insure shape retention, do so for standard armholes, raglan sleeve armholes, and the shoulder and underarm areas of kimono sleeves.

Skirts

Skirts—whether separate, joined to a bodice, or cut-in-one with the bodice—all may need subtle refinements of fit in the fashion fabric, even though you built the necessary proportions into the pattern before cutting. The fitting techniques for waist and hip fit apply to pants as well as skirts. Should your fashion include pleats, see pages 74–75; if it includes gathers, see page 75.

Fabric may require additional considerations—soft or stretchy fabrics may need to be taken in, while crisp or heavy fabrics may need to be let out. Medium to heavy-weight fabrics and interfacing may use up some wearing ease too. Skirts and pants usually have at least 1″ more ease at the waist seamline than the bodice or waistband seamline; this compensates for the abrupt hip curves just below the seam. Do not be concerned about the hemline now—your major aim should be proportion and fit.

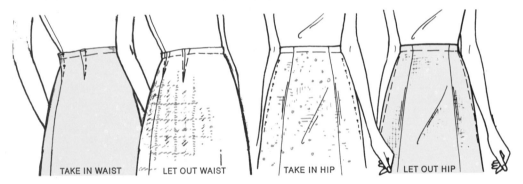

TAKE IN WAIST · LET OUT WAIST · TAKE IN HIP · LET OUT HIP

WAIST AND HIPS: To *take in waist,* divide the amount of change by the number of darts and/or seams; adjust each, tapering smoothly; avoid too much cupping. To *let out waist,* divide the amount of change by the number of darts and/or seams; adjust each, tapering smoothly. To *take in hip area only,* adjust the seams, pinning out excess fabric. To *let out hip area only,* let out each seam. Baste fitted skirt and bodice together; check the waist seam (pages 69–71). (See illustrations above.)

SWAY BACK: Even though your pattern was altered, this problem may still be evident in soft fabrics. Skirt wrinkles across the back just below the waist. To fit, lift the skirt back, making seam allowances wider at the center back and tapering into the original width at the sides. Re-shape any darts to fit your body contour. This fitting change cannot be made after a cut-in-one bodice and skirt has been cut out.

LARGE BUTTOCKS: Firm and heavy fabrics may emphasize this figure problem. The skirt back rides up and pulls side seams. To fit, lower skirt back, making seam allowance narrower across center back, tapering to original width at sides. Let out back at seams for greater circumference. Shorten and re-shape darts to fit. Only minimal fitting can be done in a cut-in-one bodice and skirt that has been cut out: darts and seams can be let out and darts re-shaped.

LARGE ABDOMEN: Crisp and heavy fabrics may emphasize this figure flaw. The front rides up and pulls side seams. To fit, lower the front, making seam allowance narrower across center front and tapering to the original width at side seams. Let out the front at side seams if greater circumference is needed; shorten and re-shape darts to fit. Only minimal fitting can be done at front darts and side seams in a cut-in-one bodice and skirt that has been cut out.

PROTRUDING HIP BONES: Usually noticed only in fitted garments, the fabric pulls across the front due to bone structure. Crisp and heavy fabrics may accent the figure flaw. To fit, re-position and re-shape darts over hip bones; if a larger circumference is needed, let out the front at side seams. A cut-in-one bodice and skirt that has been cut out cannot be fitted as well as a waist-seamed garment. Re-position and re-shape darts, letting out seams slightly.

FLAT BUTTOCKS: More visible in soft fabric, the skirt collapses when not supported by body. To fit, make darts shallower; smooth excess fabric toward side seams, making back side seam allowances wider and retaining waist fit across back. For à cut-in-one bodice and skirt, make darts shallower in skirt area and work out excess fabric at sides or back seams. Take in center back seam slightly, if you find that further correction is needed.

ONE HIGH HIP: This figure flaw in a fitted garment pulls the skirt off-grain. You may need to use a narrower seam allowance on the high hip side and a wider one on the other side to align the grain. Adjust dart length if necessary. This change cannot be made in a cut-in-one bodice and skirt after it has been cut out.

Pants

Today, pants wardrobes include casual, tailored, and frankly luxurious pants that add fashion to active lives. Do not think of your pants as an isolated item when fitting them. If your pants project does not include a top, try on some of your favorite blouses, sweaters, and jackets in varying lengths—and some fashion accessories, too.

If getting a good fit in pants has been a problem for you, do not cut into your fashion fabric until you have made a muslin pants fitting shell following the instructions in Book II. If you have had the unhappy experience of having pants fit in one fabric, but not in another, read about cutting wider seam allowances (page 58–59).

Before starting your fitting session, put on the shoes and undergarments you plan to wear with your finished garment. Remember, most girdles have a tendency to flatten your derrière—this will affect hip and crotch fit. Should your design include pockets, make sure you allow for their bulk; inside pockets—if you plan to use them—require a little more ease. Since hems are the last area to be completed, the hemline can still be changed at that point—think only of proportion and fit now.

With your pants fastened smoothly and securely, test for comfort (page 54) and evaluate the hang of the pants to see that the grain and side seams are straight (page 55); to use a plumb line, see page 18.

WAIST AND HIP: These areas are fitted in pants exactly as they are in skirts; analyze your pants first to see how the fabric reacts to your body contours. *Sway back, large buttocks, large abdomen, protruding hip bones, flat buttocks,* and *one high hip* may cause wrinkles or pulling in your fashion fabric even though you made your pattern adjustments and alterations before cutting out the fabric.

CROTCH AND INSEAM: The front and back should not be tight or baggy; the inseam area should not be pulled.
To eliminate bagginess, take in the inseam. This shortens the crotch curves, so re-baste both seams. Try on pants, as you may have to shape the crotch seam a little more. *To relieve tightness,* let out inseam. This lengthens crotch curve; re-baste seams. Try on pants, as the crotch may require a narrower seam allowance.

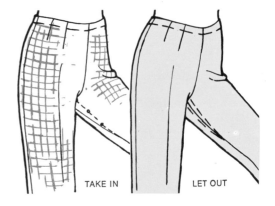

TAKE IN   LET OUT

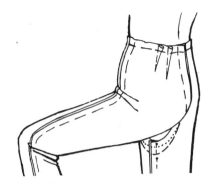

To fit wider crotch seam allowances (page 59), leave the crotch and inseam area unbasted. Fit all other areas of your pants *right side out*. Remove the pants and fit the crotch and upper inseam area *wrong side out*. Smooth fabric into position, remembering to allow ample length when standing or sitting. Mark new crotch seam. Remove pants, baste seams, and try on again right side out before stitching pants permanently together.

The Waist Area

The waist area of all garments is related closely to the midriff and hip fit, as it is the starting point from which both are created. Hip fit is discussed thoroughly in the section on skirts (pages 66–68). At this time, concentrate on the waist; this will include bodices, waistbands, and their joining to a skirt or pants. Some of these procedures can be applied to the waist and midriff areas of a darted or seamed bodice that has been cut-in-one with the skirt or pants, or any garment lacking a seam that encircles the body near the waist (i.e. a princess or shift dress, or a jumpsuit).

Since you carefully built into the pattern pieces any necessary circumference adjustments, checking the waist fit at this point will not be difficult. The character of your fashion fabric may require a minor change—soft or stretchy fabrics may need to be taken in, while crisp or firm fabrics may need to be let out. Remember, the bulk of a pleated or gathered skirt will use up wearing ease when joined to a bodice—be careful not to over-fit.

WAIST AND MIDRIFF: To *take in* waist, simply adjust the seams, taking in the side or other seams to fit the midriff and waist. Or, divide the amount of change by the number of darts and/or seams; adjust each, tapering smoothly and making sure you do not create too much cupping over the bust and back. To *let out,* simply let out the side or other seams to fit the midriff and waist of your garment. Or, divide the amount of change by the number of darts and/or seams and then adjust each, tapering smoothly.

In a cut-in-one bodice and skirt or pants, the shaping must be close to your needs, as you cannot now change it much. Fit bodice from waist working up as suggested in waist and midriff fit (above), then fit the skirt or pants section hips from the waist working down.

If you are making a jacket or coat, repeat any changes in the lining.

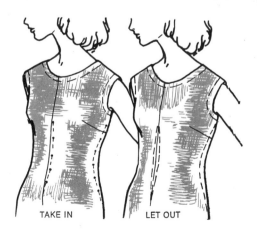

TAKE IN   LET OUT

69

WAIST SEAM: The seam that is the easiest one to evaluate on your garment is the one that falls at your waist. A raised or lowered waist seam should fall on the body as the designer originally planned, and should be fitted along with the midriff or hip area of your garment. Waist seams also give you an opportunity to adjust the hang of the skirt (or pants) and to slightly adapt the bodice length. To adjust the bodice length to your needs, simply raise or lower the garment's waist seamline.

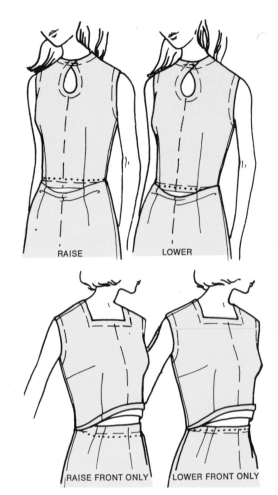

RAISE   LOWER

RAISE FRONT ONLY   LOWER FRONT ONLY

To improve the hang of your skirt or pants, it may be necessary to raise or lower waist in front or back, or along its entire circumference.

Either procedure may require slight re-shaping or re-spacing of darts. Cut-in-one bodice and skirts or pants cannot be changed in length at the waist for a more evenly hanging skirt or pants.

OTHER WAISTLINE FEATURES: A straight or contoured waistband will be stitched to the top edge of skirts and pants, while jackets and blouses may have one of these finishes applied to the bottom edge. You will also find inset bands at the waist between the bodice and the skirt or pants (page 72); or, your design may have an invisible facing on a blouse, skirt, or pants. There are also elasticized waist finishes which are quite comfortable, especially if you tend to gain and lose a small amount of weight regularly. Your fabric choice can be the decisive element in determining whether your fashion will fit as you intended.

With interfacing basted in place, fit the waistband. Fold a *straight waistband* in half lengthwise, or pin all fabric layers of a *contour waistband* together after basting the seams. First fit the waistband without the garment; place it on the body where it will fall when completed. Increase or decrease circumference as needed, allowing for bulk and being careful not to over-fit. Then fit it with the garment as explained for a waist seam.

Knits or other stretchy or loosely woven fabrics may need to be reinforced with tape to prevent their stretching at the waist seam. The support of interfacing may also be required. If you find that the waistband on your garment is curling or drooping, fit it with interfacing for greater stability and attractiveness.

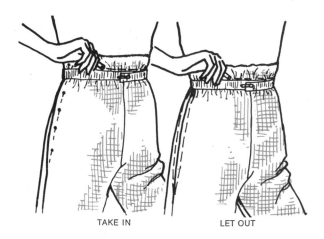

TAKE IN   LET OUT

To fit an *elasticized waist finish,* put on your garment and pin the elastic around your waist. Pull up the extension and analyze the waist and hip area. (If making pants, the crotch area should already be positioned correctly.) To fit, take in or let out as needed, making sure to leave enough room to put on and take off the garment easily. Mark your garment along the upper edge of the elastic and use this line for the foldline of the casing.

Making Fit Permanent

You must stitch darts, seams, etc. with the same care given them in fitting. At the sewing machine, you can very easily over-handle your fabric by stretching the seams. You can also distort the grain if there is too much pressure on the presser foot. The use of your iron and your pressing habits may mar fabric. Improper storage between fittings can also wrinkle, stretch, and distort the garment, necessitating a re-fitting.

- ☐ Trim widened seam allowances to ⅝"; extend narrow ones as suggested on page 56.
- ☐ Reinforce supporting seams in stretchy fabrics with tape; shoulder seams with ribbon seam binding; and neck edges with stretched bias tape shaped to match garment contour. The tape will be stitched in place permanently as you join the seam.
- ☐ Attach interfacing permanently to underlining or baste securely.
- ☐ Press as you sew: press straight seams on a flat surface, and curved seams and darts over a rounded surface.
- ☐ Protect fabric from imprints on the right side by using a seam roll, brown paper, and other appropriate equipment.
- ☐ Clip seam allowances so they will lie flat, or notch them to remove excess fabric and eliminate bulk.
- ☐ Store garments between fittings on your dress form or use a padded hanger and hang garment where it will not be wrinkled. Stretchy fabrics should be folded with tissue paper or laid out flat.
- ☐ Pin the closures shut as carefully as you did during the fitting. Use pins cautiously if they will be in place for an extended period of time, as they may leave imprints on the fabric.
- ☐ Pin armhole and neckline seam allowances to your dress form or to a hanger covered with a wide section of muslin.
- ☐ Pin a skirt's waist seamline to the dress form or to a hanger.
- ☐ Fold pants, matching side and inseams, and place over the padded bar of a hanger or a clip hanger. Pin pants to your dress form along the seamline in the same way.

Design Features

What do you do when fitting a garment that has bands, pleats, vents, tucks, gathers, or pockets? How do you fit an ensemble that includes two or more garments that are to be worn in layers, one over the other? What do you do when you want to use a bulky lining? These are questions every woman who sews asks at one time or another. You may be one of the lucky few who chose a fabric for your design which will have no involved fitting—these design features will neither droop nor cause the garment to feel a little snug. Here, Vogue Patterns will give you guidance in draping your fabric beautifully over your body contours.

Inset Bands and Cowls

Decorative seaming details that are a part of the garment shell style lines must be basted in place before your first try-on. Of self- or contrasting fashion fabric, bands can be curved strips of equal width used at neck, armholes, or opening edges; straight or shaped strips used at the waist; or straight strips of equal width used to finish the hem edges of sleeves, shirts, or pants. Of self-fabric, a cowl has soft draping folds created by its bias cut.

To prepare the garment shell for a fitting, baste each detail section to its corresponding garment section, lapping inner edges and matching seamlines. Baste garment shell together. When satisfied with the fit, stitch bands permanently (see pages 241–242 of The Vogue Sewing Book for construction tips).

BANDS: Maintain a uniform finished width for the entire length of a band at **neck** and **armhole edges**. Should you make any fitting changes in these areas, adjust band seamlines accordingly.

Inset bands at the **waist** are basted to the bodice and skirt or pants. When fitting, allow for later fabric bulk; do not over-fit. For soft fabrics, underline an inset section that must support a full skirt.

Bands used as a hem finish influence the length and drape of your fabric, so consider total garment length before cutting fabric. If your hem band is doubled, join its ends and fold it wrong sides together. Lap and baste band to garment; raise, lower, increase, or decrease as needed.

COWLS: The secret of a beautifully draped cowl is to make a stay cut on the straight grain, using your master pattern (pages 183–185) as a guide. Cut stay from lining fabric; then construct, finishing the neck edge with a narrow binding. Baste stay to cowl along the outer edges, easing the cowl to fit; avoid stretching. Baste cowl in place; lap its edge over garment and match seamlines.

Mold and shape your cowl on a dress form, basting back edges together as they fall. It is recommended that you use weights, if necessary, to control the drape of the cowl.

Pleats, Vents, Tucks, and Gathers

Carefully controlled fullness is the rationale behind designers' use of pleats, vents, tucks, and gathers. Aesthetically, these design features add visual interest and dimension, and practically, they allow extra room for mobility and comfort. Any woman can wear each of these four design elements successfully if she has first analyzed her figure to gain an understanding of how much controlled fullness is flattering to her, and where to use it to best advantage.

Pleats are folds of fabric which may be sharply pressed or softly rolled with no pressing; they may be edgestitched along the fold for a defined silhouette or they may be left to fall freely with no stitching. Vents are two fabric layers with an opening; they allow for action, and then return to their original position where they are usually inconspicuous. Tucks can be stitched on either the inside or outside of the garment, and can be a decorative as well as a functional design feature; they can be found over body contours, or released at one or both ends to add design fullness. Gathers are the simplest means by which controlled fullness can be incorporated in a design. They can be skimpy and hang straight, or they can be full, billowy, and stand away from the body. Whatever form controlled fullness takes in your garment, there is an easy way to adapt the fabric to your needs. Success with these design features begins with accurate markings and accurate bastings to make fitting easier.

PLEATS: Single pleats or clusters of pleats used as a focal point do not present problems, as these are never fitted—the fitting is done in the other vertical seams. However, should a single pleat include an underlay and incorporate the closure, simply increase or decrease circumference by taking in or letting out at the foldline or roll line. Use a wider or narrower seam allowance on the pleat extension.

Careful planning is needed for *all-around pleats,* as might be found in a skirt. Complete the hem before basting the pleats in place. Then form the pleats from the hem up. This takes the guesswork out of fitting—any unwanted length can be worked out at the waist or other seam in which they will be joined. Circumference adjustment will be required if pleats sag and overlap, or if they twist and pull.

TAKE IN   LET OUT

To adjust garment circumference at this time, release only one pleat to see the extent of the change needed; take in or let out that one pleat until the skirt fits correctly. Remove the skirt and divide the amount of change equally among all of the pleats. The secret of fitting straight pleats is to retain the original foldlines or roll lines by making any changes along the indicated placement lines.

Pleats can also be fitted for waist and hip circumference. Fit the waist, tapering to hip or fit the hip, tapering to waist; or, fit to accommodate both circumferences. Naturally, the pleats will become deeper or narrower when the hip area requires fitting. Shaped pleats whose upper portion has been cut away to reduce bulk can be fitted similarly.

When your garment's pleats have been fitted to your satisfaction, machine baste along the waist seamline to secure the folds, seam allowances, and/or the underlaps. Pleats that are to be permanently creased should be pressed at this time. Soft pleats should be steam-pressed while pinned to your dress form and smoothed gently by hand to drape nicely. Remove all basting except at the waist seamline and then try on your garment again.

Pleats should hang straight without spreading or overlapping. If they do either, raise or lower the seamline until pleats hang correctly. Join the pleats to the other section at new seamline.

OVERLAPPING   CORRECT   SPREADING

LOWER   RAISE

VENTS: This is an opening formed by an overlapped edge and an underlapped edge; it is found at the end of a seam. A vent will require fitting if it spreads or twists. Be sure the upper ends of the vent are supported properly before you begin. If the circumference needs to be adjusted through the vent area of the garment, the vent edges will become correspondingly deeper or narrower. Taper any changes above the vent gradually to the garment seamline; the garment above the vent must be smooth for the vent to lie flat.

TAKE IN   LET OUT

TUCKS: These may need fitting attention, especially if they are over body contours or are controlling circumference. Simply divide the amount of change needed by the number of tucks; increase or decrease tuck width accordingly.

GATHERS: Your fabric choice will play an important role in the performance of your gathers. Crisp or lightweight fabrics may billow too much over the hips, while stiff or heavyweight fabric may cup and fall into awkward folds. How the fabric reacts to the gathers and your figure must be discerned at this point. If needed, you can fit out some of the excess at each seam or you can dart it out at the waist. Darting it out will not affect the sweep of the skirt, and is the best technique when the gathers form excessive bulk at the seam. Space long darts evenly throughout the skirt at the waist. When the desired effect has been achieved, stitch the darts permanently; trim to $5/8''$, and press open, then form gathers. For stiff or heavy fabrics, it may be necessary to reduce the skirt sweep to maintain the silhouette. Fit out excess at each seam for desired effect.

Pocket Placement

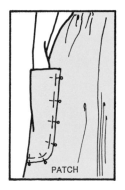 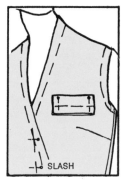 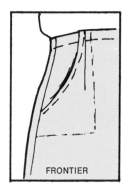 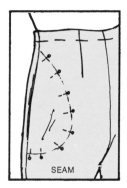

Pockets are decorative and functional, and add an extra bit of fashion dash to the garments they adorn. Patch pockets are applied to the garment surface; buttonhole, welt, or flap pockets are inserted into a slash with an inside pocket section cut of lining or lightweight fabric. Frontier pockets have a self-fabric facing; one of the pocket layers is cut of fashion fabric and is part of the garment shell. The pocket hidden in a seam is a convenience feature. Functional pockets positioned below the waist should be placed where your hands can slip into them comfortably and should be deep enough for your hands. Pockets above the waist are usually decorative; place them where they will be most flattering and balanced. Curvaceous women should generally avoid flap or patch pockets. Eliminate a pocket or pare down its proportions to make the most of you while still maintaining attractive dimensions.

Before placing pockets, any fitting changes in your garment should be resolved. Thread trace grainlines, so you will be able to align the grain of the pocket, welt, or flap with the grain of your garment. Turn in seam allowances of a patch pocket, welt, or flap; baste. A frontier pocket is part of the garment shell and must be basted in place for the first fitting. Baste shaped edges of pocket and garment together, and baste side and waist edges together along seamline before a fitting. A garment with inside pocket sections requires more wearing ease so the pockets will not leave a ridge or an outline on the garment. Pin patch pockets, flaps, or welts over placement markings, keeping grains aligned. Do not hesitate to shift them to a more flattering position.

Pockets should lie flat and smooth, and should not gape open. If a pocket is placed over a body contour, pin it in place carefully so that it is slightly curved over the body. Do not baste it taut, as this will distort the fit of the garment.

Garments having pockets that are set into seams need enough extra ease for the pocket and your hand. Their placement must be planned before the garment is cut out. In medium to heavyweight fabrics, do not over-fit, as the pocket may gape open due to lack of wearing ease. These pockets should be invisible; the opening should lie flat and smooth. When your garment is made from a stretchy fabric or cut on the bias, reinforce foldlines and placement lines with tape to prevent stretching.

Pockets in *pants* of all styles add serviceability. The pockets must be strategically placed so that they do not add extra width across the hipline or derrière.

Pocket placement in **knits** depends on the character of the fabric with which you are working. Though there is great diversity in knits, some of the characteristic drape and performance are not predictable, and it is here that we must issue a word of caution about pockets: make sure you do not over-fit, as pocket imprints will show through. In the stable knits, most pocket treatments are appropriate. In moderate stretch or stretch knits, where there must be give on the body, it is often best to avoid pockets. Patch pockets on stretchy knits are feasible only if you fit them carefully to the garment over your body contours.

Layered Fitting

It is essential that you have a thorough understanding of wearing ease and style ease because the key to fitting layered garments lies in these concepts. If you need a refresher, see pages 25–30. Layering demands consideration when choosing your pattern **before** cutting into your fashion fabric and **again** when fitting. The relationship of each fabric layer and its reaction to the layer that precedes it on the body is variable. A simple costume (a ribbed, bulky blouse with jacket and skirt or pants) or an ensemble (blouse, vest, jacket, coat, shorts, and skirt) should be fitted from the body out. You need not compromise comfort for fit.

Garments presented in the Vogue Patterns catalogue as a total layered look have built-in wearing ease for each layer. Jacket and coat patterns have the extra ease so they can be worn over other garments—unless made from extremely heavy or bulky fabrics. However, a jacket that is a cut-off version of a coat cannot be worn under the coat, as the two have the same wearing ease. Likewise, separates chosen at random to make up a layered ensemble need special consideration, as they may not have been created to work as you plan to use them. Cut wider seam allowances (pages 58–59) to build a safety factor into your fabric. When fitting start with the layer closest to the body and work outward. With each additional layer, the amount of ease will be slightly greater to accommodate the previous layers. If a bulky lining or interlining is included, read the next page before you begin cutting out and fitting your fabric to your needs.

When fitting layered garments, be sure not to fit out the wearing ease and be constantly aware of your fashion silhouette to avoid over-fitting and loss of style lines. Layered fitting pertains not only to cold weather ensembles, but also includes swimsuits with succeeding layers of cover-up fashions in easy-care fabrics.

Bulky Linings

Adding bulky linings to outerwear provides a luxurious finish as well as added comfort and warmth. Bulky linings can be decorative as well as insulating and are often added to coats, suits, jackets, and toppers. When one thinks of bulky linings, fur or fur-like fabrics immediately jump into mind, but there are other types too, such as quilted satin, satin laminated with foam or wool-like fibers, or standard linings interlined with lamb's wool. Even brushed cotton flannels teamed with denim produce unexpectedly warm sportswear jackets. Whatever fashion impression you wish to make, there is a bulky lining that will accomplish it.

Choose fabric for bulky lining that is compatible with your fashion fabric in care requirements; it should also be shrink resistant. The weight and bulk of the lining requires an outer fabric that will not collapse. Cut wider seam allowances in both your lining and the fashion fabric to allow for fitting (see pages 58–59). Unlike traditional linings, where the garment is constructed and then the lining is fitted, a **bulky lining is fitted first,** then the outer garment is fitted. Place right sides of your bulky lining next to the body. If it is part of an ensemble, fit the bulky lining over the previous garment layer.

Pin the shoulders together; while fitting, it should not slide off the shoulder line. Remember, long-haired furs and fakes take up more wearing ease than short-haired ones do. Note: The sleeves of any bulky lining are preferably cut from a lightweight fabric.

AT THE CLOSE of this chapter on fitting, let us stop briefly to reconsider the new relationships and skills that you have added to your fitting repertoire and then take a glance at what is to come. We have examined in depth the standards of good fit and applied them to any fabric and garment you might select. We put your future garment into new perspective with an analysis of accessories, notions, and findings. Then, you actually began to assemble your garment, first basting the garment shell together to determine the extent of minor changes needed. At this point, your garment shell should be stitched permanently with perfect fit incorporated. In the next chapter, we shall focus on fitting specialized garment details that make your creation no longer a garment shell, but an expression of your life style and fashion direction. We anticipate that not only is a happy ending in sight for you in our fitting story but also a new beginning in your appreciation of the art of fitting.

A Fitting Finale

In carefully fitting each area of your garment, you have given your fashion fabric the dimensions needed to bring wearing ease and style ease into perspective. You have laid the foundation for a superbly fitted garment. But before you add the remaining fashion items that will make your garment unique—facings, collars, sleeves, and linings—pause at this point to evaluate your progress. Stand before a full length mirror and scrutinize each of the following aspects of your garment shell:

- ☐ Fabric grain is balanced on both halves of the garment shell.
- ☐ Underlining and interfacing do not have bubbles or wrinkles.
- ☐ Shoulder seams or darts are in their correct position.
- ☐ Necklines hug the body and are smooth and flat.
- ☐ Bodice darts or seam details hug bust as designer intended.
- ☐ Bodice back molds smoothly over the shoulders and entire back.
- ☐ Waist area is wrinkle-free and fits as intended by designer.
- ☐ Hip fit—in both front and back—is smooth and wrinkle-free.
- ☐ Pleats, gathers, and vents are smooth, flat, and hang correctly.
- ☐ Blouse, jacket, and coat shells fit with adequate ease over any garments with which they will be worn.
- ☐ Pants have adequate ease in crotch area and lie smoothly.

Should you detect a problem—an undesirable wrinkle caused during stitching your garment shell permanently; a seam that does not lie flat; or a dart that appears too bulky—do not hesitate to make a change at this time. Review page 71, then release stitching and smooth fabric into position; baste securely and re-stitch. Or, trim excess bulk from darts, press them open, and re-stitch seam.

Focus On The Fine Points

Once you have determined the fit of the body of your garment, there are few fitting surprises left. From now on the going will be easy, because you know what to look for and are armed with knowledge of the fine points of specific changes to be made. You also have a repertoire of construction and pressing techniques found in The Vogue Sewing Book. These last refinements in fit generally involve clean finishing and greater fashion emphasis on facings, closures, collars, sleeves, sleeve finishes, pleats, and vents. The sleek elegance of a lining inside your garment must be considered now. Also in this section, you will finish garment edges and insure shape and fit for the life of your garment.

Facings

The fit of a facing should be smooth and flat so that the faced area has little bulk. It should be reinforced with interfacing and may be taped to reduce the chances of stretching. In addition to a flat, smooth fit, you should strive for durability. Facings can be found at the neckline, armholes, waistline, and sometimes at the hemlines of sleeves and skirts. Before fitting, make any changes in the facing that have been made in the garment. If you have raised or lowered the neckline, adjusted the shoulder seam and the underarm area, or raised or lowered the waist seamline, transfer these changes to the facing. Baste the facing to the inside of the garment, wrong sides together, and try on. Make any changes needed to adapt your fashion fabric.

Neckline edges may require clipping at even intervals in order for them to fit, while *armhole* edges may require that only the underarm curve be clipped. When fitting a *waist* facing on a skirt or on pants, ease the garment to the facing as indicated by your pattern. Strive for a smooth fit over the hips.

When fitting *knitted* or *stretch* fabrics, avoid over-handling them. If you find, in *heavy* or *bulky* fabrics, that facings leave a ridge or imprint on the outside of your garment, replace the self-fabric facing with one of lightweight fabric.

If your fashion garment includes a collar or other features sandwiched between the garment and facing, this must be fitted before you attach the facing permanently. The same applies to a facing that finishes a closure edge. You must fit the collar, then the facing, as any change will affect all three garment areas.

Closures

Before making a closure permanent, it requires close evaluation. Not only must a closure be smooth and flat, but the items—zippers, buttons, snaps, decorative closures—must work with your fashion fabric without overwhelming the garment or pulling the closure out of line. If your closure includes a facing, it must be fitted at the same time. Baste applied facings in place as instructed above. Turn extended facings inside along foldlines; baste neck edges together and along the foldline.

ZIPPERS: Baste zipper to garment by your chosen method of application and try on the garment. The closure must lie smoothly and be flat; its weight should not distort the fabric. Make sure the length is appropriate for your figure—replace the zipper with another length if it ends at an awkward area; move a side zipper to a center front or back seam in a skirt or pants if your hip curves look asymmetrical.

For stretchy or bias fabrics, stabilize opening edges with stretched bias tape (ribbon seam binding is usually too rigid for these edges).

To insert a zipper in *stretchable knits,* pin the opening edges to the zipper tape while the garment is in its stretched condition on your body. Remove garment and baste securely for a test fit—the zipper area may wrinkle or twist when the fabic is relaxed, but it will fit perfectly when the garment is worn.

MEETING EDGES: Baste and pin edges to tape as you did for fitting, page 53. Then baste the closure in position to make sure it will not distort the fabric or style lines. When fitting knits, expect stable knits to support almost any closure, but moderate stretch knits may require a closure that is lighter in weight and more flexible.

Since most stretchable unbonded knits do not usually have closures other than zippers, they require a special technique for fitting (see zippers, page 80).

OVERLAPS: Lap opening edges, matching centers, and pin together at closure markings. Re-position buttonhole or other closure markings so they fall at bust, waist, and hip; this prevents the opening from gaping over your contours. Baste closures in place to see how they react with the fabric. Remember, you can always substitute smaller buttons (increasing their number), but your lap will not take larger buttons because the extension beyond the center was planned for a specific button size. Re-space markings evenly if changed. Mark where a snap or hook is needed to support opening edges. *Caution:* These closures should not be made final at this time if a collar will be part of the garment. Fit your collar as instructed on this page and pages 82–83. Then determine the position markings for your buttons or other closures. Pay special attention to asymmetrical closures. Securely pin along center lines and avoid over-handling. Stay edges with stretched bias tape if needed. Test weight and flexibility of closures to avoid distortion.

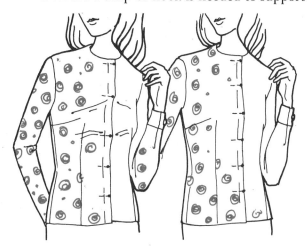

Collars

Careful fitting can create a collar that is a fashion highlight and an expression of the best of your sewing abilities. It is important that you maintain the same fitting standards—whether your collar is a shape variation of the flat, rolled, or standing collar, or is a combination of two, like a notched or shawl collar.

If collar construction and shaping have been one of your problems, review pages 244–257 and 343–348 in The Vogue Sewing Book. You must build the right amount of fabric into the collar so the upper collar will roll smoothly over the undercollar. This will result in a finished collar that lies softly on the garment without curling; the seam will be invisible along the outer edges, and the collar will rise gently from the garment neckline.

Your garment shell plays a most important part in a successfully fitted collar. Be sure to check any changes you have made in the shoulder and neck areas of your garment. If you raised or lowered the neckline, or adjusted the shoulder or back, the neck seamline circumference may be larger or smaller than that of the collar. Measure along the marked neck seamlines on the garment and the original neck seamline on the collar. Should there be any discrepancy, correct the collar as follows:

For fitting changes of *less than 1″*, ease the collar slightly to the garment, or ease the garment slightly to the collar; this should not affect the rise and roll of the collar. Baste and test (see page 82); since the change recommended is less than ¼″ on each quarter of the neck seamline, it should result in a well-fitted collar. However, if your fabric is stiff, crisp, or bulky, and does not ease well as you shrink out the fullness, the depth of the seam allowance may be adjusted on the collar until it fits properly.

For fitting changes of *1" or more,* cut the collar in muslin and test-fit before cutting your fashion fabric. Increase or decrease the length of muslin collar so all position markings match at centers and shoulders. Transfer changes to pattern, then cut and construct the fashion fabric collar, testing as explained below.

Many collars are prepared, then sandwiched between the garment and facing. Others have an undercollar stitched to the garment, an upper collar stitched to the facing, and then are joined to the garment's outer edges. A third type of collar finishes the garment edge without a facing.

To fit a finished collar, lap the collar neck edge over the garment, matching seamlines, centers, and shoulders. Try on the garment or put it on your dress form to fit. Use the pattern envelope illustration as a guide to check the appearance of the collar. The collar should lie symmetrically against both halves of the garment at the closing and where a two-section collar meets.

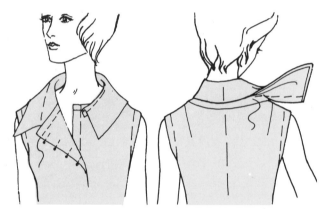

A ROLLED collar can hug the neck or stand away from it, but the fit is the same. The roll should smoothly and evenly encircle the neck; it should not ride high or low, and the finished edge of the collar should cover the back neck seamline. Fit to your satisfaction; mark established roll line and any changes. Check closures (pages 80–81) before removing collar.

A NOTCHED or convertible collar begins to shape from the top buttonhole marking. Adjust at the neck seamlines if needed. The finished collar edge should cover the back neck seamline. To check the closed position when collar ends meet, turn in the corner of the overlap as illustrated. The ends will then lie smoothly and you can test the fit. When satisfied with the fit, mark the roll on both collar and lapels. Then turn to pages 80–81 for information on fitting the closure. Always allow for the roll of the lapels when you fit either the applied or the extended type of facing.

A FLAT collar is one of the basic collar styles from which all others are derived. It may require clipping at even intervals to appear as it should. Mark any changes on the neckline and then remove the collar from the garment.

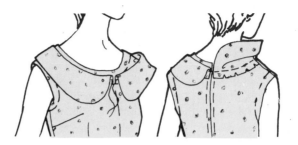

A STANDING collar can be crisp and military, or it can be a molded bias one that turns down over itself. The *crisp* standing collar is applied to the garment and adjusted until it fits correctly; clip seam allowances if necessary; remember that the inner layer is usually used to finish the neck seam. Mark changes in seamlines before removing. The finished edge of the *bias* standing collar should be turned down so that it just covers the neck seamline. Stretch collar gently to mold smoothly. Baste along the established roll through all thicknesses; mark seamline changes before removing the collar.

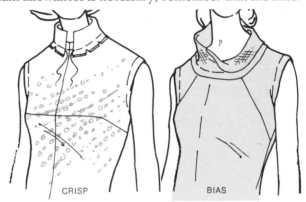

CRISP   BIAS

A collar whose UNDERCOLLAR is sewn to the garment and whose UPPER COLLAR is sewn to the facing is handled as follows. Lap and baste the undercollar to the garment. Begin the roll for the collar and/or lapels as indicated in the pattern illustration for your design. Roll the collar smoothly and make sure the collar seamline will fall just below the back neck seamline. Mark the roll and any seamline

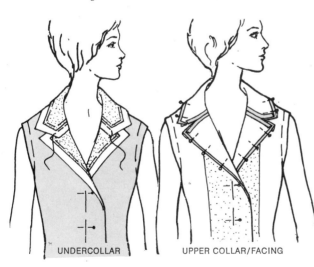

UNDERCOLLAR   UPPER COLLAR/FACING

changes; remove collar. Stitch the undercollar to the garment permanently. Then baste the facing unit together, lapping and basting the upper collar to its neck edge if there is a separate section. Place collar and facing unit over garment, matching neck seamlines; baste. With your garment *wrong side out*, fit the collar and facing to the garment, shaping carefully along the established roll. Mark any changes in seamline of upper collar and facing before removing.

Pockets

Now you must take a final look to make certain that the finished pocket is perfect on the garment. The small details involved add up to a fashion garment of which you can be proud. Check the flap or welt and make sure that it is flat and smooth. If the edges of a flap turn up, they can be tacked securely in place for about ½″ from the top; take care that the stitching does not show on the outside. The garment must have enough wearing ease in the pocket area to accommodate the pocket type—patch, those inserted in a slash, frontier, or in-seam. Pockets should curve smoothly over the body with the garment; there should be no pulls or puckers in the garment around the pocket.

If you plan to add a decorative button or buckle, check to see that its weight can be supported by the pocket without distorting the shape or opening. At this time, a little spot pressing will make your pockets crisp and fresh; steam-press on the dress form, shrinking out any slightly stretched areas of the pocket opening.

Pleats

After your pleats or vents have been made final and everything has been stitched permanently, you may find that your pleats or vents still require some refinement. If you feel that the pleats need **edgestitching** to hold a sharp crease, do this before joining them to the garment or waistband and after completing the hem. If your fashion fabric needs some additional help to support the weight of the pleats, shape a stay of underlining or other lightweight, durable fabric; refer to The Vogue Sewing Book for detailed information on the construction techniques of pleats.

Set-in Sleeves

To perfect fitting techniques for a set-in sleeve, your approach must combine confidence with flexibility. With the knowledge and control you have attained in making your muslin fitting shell, it will be simple to set the sleeve into your finalized garment shell—regardless of your fabric choice. The sleeve should join the bodice just over the shoulder bone and fall smoothly, without pulls or strain, around the armhole. Its cap should cup smoothly, the arm portion should not wrinkle below the cupping, and the underarm seam should fall about 1″ below the armpit. Since all your personal adjustments were built into the pattern pieces before you cut out your fashion fabric, the main concern now is adapting the sleeve as your fabric dictates.

PREPARE SLEEVES: Baste any elbow darts or adjust ease as you baste each sleeve seam. Ease threads can be added to the sleeve cap by hand or machine, depending on your fabric. Turn up the hem along proposed hemline and pin, or apply any sleeve finish that will affect the sleeve length (see pages 86–87).

Pin the sleeve section to the armhole and adjust ease; fasten the ease thread ends securely and then baste the sleeve in position for a fitting. *Do not* shrink the sleeve cap at this time. If you need to refresh your memory about correctly setting in a sleeve, see pages 259–261 in The Vogue Sewing Book.

To fit the sleeves, first check comfort (page 54) and grain (page 55), then check sleeve fit from armhole to hem. If a loosely woven or knitted fabric is a trifle big, **take in** the sleeve a bit; in a bulky fashion fabric, you may **let out** the sleeve a bit if it is too snug. Taper any changes to the original armhole seamline. In a long sleeve without an opening, be sure that you have allowed enough room for your hand to slip through easily.

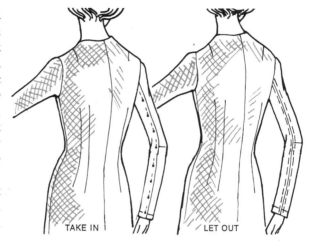

Check sleeve cap, shoulder, and underarm areas. If *distribution of ease* in sleeve cap is not correct, see page 146. You must eliminate some *excess ease* from fabrics that will not smooth out to your satisfaction; these include durable press and synthetics treated for easy care. Fit the sleeve cap as explained on page 147. Remove the sleeve, then re-cut the cap area, using your altered pattern. Re-set the sleeve into the garment to test the change in ease.

When working with bulky, heavy, stiff, tightly woven, or textured fabrics, the sleeve cap sometimes requires special handling. Un-pin the sleeve cap after the ease threads have been fastened securely, and place garment on your dress form. Turn in the seam allow-

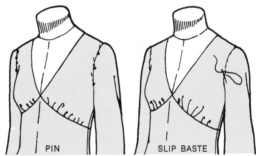

ance along ease threads and shape the sleeve cap smoothly; pin the sleeve cap in place as you work. Slip baste the sleeve cap into position while the garment is on the dress form and test for proper fit and appearance before permanently stitching.

Check *shoulder length* and upper part of armhole. Raise or lower sleeve cap until sleeve cap seamline is positioned on the bodice shoulder over arm hinge. Rather than change the sleeve seam allowance, take a deeper or narrower seam allowance at bodice shoulder.

If *underarm* pulls or strains, make the same adjustment that is made for raglan sleeves, pages 64–65.

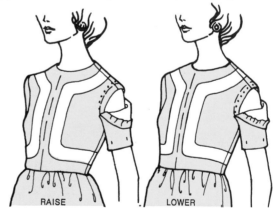

Sleeve Finishes

Many sleeve finishes will add length to your sleeve—whether set-in, raglan, or kimono—and must be in position when you are fitting. Cuffs—either turnback or extended—and applied bands are a part of the total sleeve length. Other sleeve finishes may be sandwiched between the sleeve edge and a facing; these do not affect the sleeve length, but may necessitate minor fitting at the hem.

If your sleeve has an opening that will be slashed, do not complete the opening until the sleeve has been fitted. For a sleeve with pleats or gathers, baste pleats in place and add the gathering threads so the sleeve can be adjusted to fit the finish.

To prepare cuffs or bands for a fitting, include any underlining or interfacing. Fold a cuff or band with an extended facing wrong sides together, and baste ends and upper edges along seamlines. For a two-section cuff or band, baste the layers along lower edge, then turn along basted seam. With wrong sides together, baste ends and upper edge. Lap the ends of band or cuff, matching seamlines; baste.

Lap cuff or band over sleeve, matching seamlines; baste. When ready to fit, match markings and use pins to fasten a cuff with a closure as it will be worn.

After basting sleeve into armhole (or applying the finish to or pinning up the hem of a raglan or kimono sleeve), check the fit and length of the sleeve.

TO FIT CUFFS OR BANDS, increase or decrease the *circumference* at opening edges or at the ends that were lapped; adjust the sleeve circumference to fit the finish. Do not over-fit—heavy or bulky fabrics will use up wearing ease when the cuff or band is completed; for a finish without an opening, allow enough room to slip your hand through. If the pleated or gathered area is too stiff or full, remove some fullness by eliminating a few gathers or decreasing the width of pleats; see page 75 for details.

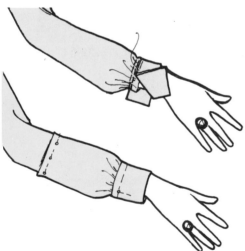

With cuff or band in place, check the *sleeve length* and design fullness. Increase or decrease the sleeve length without changing the depth of the finish unless your fabric dictates—in stiff or heavy fabrics it may be necessary to take from the seam allowance of the finish too. If these fabrics do not assume the correct silhouette when gathered or pleated, adapt the circumference as previously suggested.

Mark any changes on both the sleeve and the cuff or band finish. Remove both the sleeve and the sleeve finish from a set-in sleeve; remove the sleeve finish from a kimono or raglan sleeve that is part of your garment shell.

TO FIT OTHER SLEEVE FINISHES, check the *sleeve length.* Adjust a short, elbow, three-quarter, bracelet, or full length sleeve so the hem edge parallels the floor. Mark any changes made in hemlines or seamlines.

Linings

The lining of your fashion garment is the last layer of fabric and unit of construction. A lining that fits is an essential part of fashion perfection. If your lining fabric is not compatible with your fashion fabric, a badly shaped garment will result. It may be wise to forgo cutting out the lining until you have fitted the garment. If you have made any changes when fitting your garment, repeat these on your lining before cutting. It is a good habit to allow at least 1″ extra at lining hem edges to allow for an ample ease pleat. If you will be using a bulky lining or interlining, refer to page 78 before cutting either your fashion fabric or lining.

Coats and jackets are usually lined, and your pattern will include pieces for the lining. Dresses, skirts, and pants do not usually require a lining – if you wish to line them for luxury, durability, or comfort and need construction advice, see pages 339, 353 – 357, and 364 in The Vogue Sewing Book.

FITTING A LINING is an essential step in achieving a durable, attractive fashion. The garment should be free of wrinkles and distortion, and the lining should not cause bubbles or ridges on the surface of the fashion fabric. Ideally your lining must be a fraction smaller in circumference than the fashion garment into which it will be inserted. However, a lining that is considerably smaller in circumference will be uncomfortable, and will wear due to strain. Conversely, a lining that is too big for the garment might affect the fit because its extra bulk uses up wearing ease.

Regardless of garment style, fitting a lining is an easy feat in the completion of your garment. Because you know well the fit of your garment, you can focus quickly on any changes. Baste the lining shell together, repeating in it any changes in fit made in the garment; leave the appropriate seam open for a zipper or other closure. Linings are always pinned into the garment so the wrong sides are together. All lining centers, seams, and darts should be matched to those of the garment. Put pleats, gathers, and ease threads in the lining if the addition of these is indicated by the design of your garment.

For *skirts and pants,* place the lining shell inside the garment. Pin, matching all centers, darts, and seams; if necessary, ease garment to fit the lining at upper edge. Turn in the opening edges to clear the zipper teeth. For pants, make sure the lining crotch seam and inseams cross those of the garment exactly. Baste the upper and opening edges together and try on the garment for a fitting. Make any changes as suggested above until both layers mold together smoothly without any bubbling or pulling.

Dress linings are usually fitted immediately after the garment shell has been fitted so edges can be finished with the facings, sleeves, and collars. Place the lining shell inside garment shell; pin, matching all centers, darts, and seams. Ease garment to fit

lining at neck and armhole edges, and turn in the opening edges to clear the zipper teeth or other closures. Baste neck, armhole, and opening edges together and try on garment for a fitting. Make changes as suggested on the previous page until both layers mold together. If the fabric irritates your skin, cut facings from lining fabric, too. To line sleeves, refer to the information below on coats and jackets.

Coat and jacket linings discussed at this point are to be made from standard light- and medium weight lining fabrics. When coats or jackets are interlined, or when the lining fabric is bulky, the lining cannot be fitted successfully after the garment has been completed. Turn to page 78 for fitting directions.

When fitting a lining, you must compensate for the reaction of your lining and fashion fabrics. Baste the back pleat in place, and leave the shoulder seams open as you join the lining shell. Place lining inside garment, matching back pleat to center back marking or seam. Working toward the front edges, match seamlines and baste. Match armhole and neck seamlines. Then lap shoulder edges, again match seamlines, and baste. Try on the garment and test its fit. Shoulder pads may create excess fabric through the shoulder area of both front and back, so eliminate any wrinkles by working them out at the shoulder seam. When you see that the two layers are working as one, mark the changes and then remove the lining for con-

struction. When the lining shell has been permanently inserted into the garment, but the hem has not been sewn, you are ready to fit the sleeves.

Fitting lining sleeves demands care—they should be slightly smaller in circumference than the garment sleeves to ensure a comfortable and smooth fit in your completed fashion. Baste sleeve seams, adding any darts or ease threads at elbows. Add ease threads to sleeve caps. Insert each lining sleeve in the appropriate garment sleeve. Lap armhole edges, matching seamlines; pin, adjust ease, and baste. Shape each sleeve cap and lining sleeve inside the garment, adjusting as needed. Mark changes determined in the fitting and remove sleeve linings.

After sleeve lining has been permanently inserted in the garment, turn to page 91 for directions on completing the lining hems of both the garment and the sleeves.

An Eye For Appearance

You are now approaching that most rewarding point—the completion of your fashion sewing project. Your fashion garment fits to perfection, and only the finishing touches—hems, closures, and a touch-up pressing—remain to complete the fit and hang of your garment. These steps ensure beautifully finished hems for both garment and lining. Determining the permanent position of your garment closure—buttons, frogs, etc.—is another aspect of fitting at this time. A final gentle touch-up pressing will make your garment impeccably smooth and crisp. All of these details are crucial to the maintenance of the fit toward which you have so patiently worked, so do not underestimate their importance or lessen your efforts for perfection. Even the most unassuming of accessories can have great effect on the success of your fit.

Accessories

In checking the fit of your fashion garment during the first fittings, you were alerted to the roles that accessories play in the fit and look of your completed garment (see pages 44–45). Now you must further incorporate your accessories so that the fit of your garment will always be just right. Your accessories have been chosen for their proportion, color, and texture; they will blend or contrast to enhance your design and fabric. Now add touches from the haute couture to assure success.

Attach belt loops and carriers where needed to support the weight and maintain the position of your belt. A small thread loop inside the neckline of a dress will secure the ends of a tucked-in scarf. Try on your jewelry—pins, chains, earrings—and see if they will affect your final choice of button. Perhaps sandals or hosiery in a fashion color will necessitate a slight change in your hem length. A handbag in a contrasting color may supply an accent that will give extra lift to your creation. A bright, colorful lining can set off any number of accessory ideas. Whatever your fashion whims, now is the time to tie the ends together to form a pretty package. Remember that accessories should add focus rather than decoration to perfect fit.

Hems

Earlier in the process of fitting you had pinned up a trial hem to judge the fit and proportions of your emerging garment. Now the time has come to perfect your hem. Before you start, there are several factors to consider—the proper undergarments, shoes or boots, and any fashion accessories that will affect the proportion of the design must be worn when determining the proper length for your newly created garment. If your fashion includes a belt, wear it when working on the hem, as your garment will be shortened when the belt is secured around your body.

For centuries, hem length was dictated by fashion. Today's best hem length is one that helps to create a total and successful fashion look. A hem length must perfect the proportion of the silhouette and the drape of the fabric. Hem depth is another factor—both your height and fashion fabric influence the choice of finished hem depth. Generally, a tall woman requires a slightly deeper hem, and a short woman, a narrower hem. On a Vogue Patterns dress or coat design, a 3″ hem is usually allowed.

A very full, sheer skirt having a hemline on the straight grain can have a hem up to 10″ deep if you want it to influence the drape of the fabric. Or, a fabric like chiffon can have a narrow ⅛″ hem. A circular skirt usually calls for a hem no deeper than 1″. Jackets and pants may have a 1½″ hem; blouses may have from ⅜″ to 1½″, depending on style. In a very heavy fabric, avoid a deep hem no matter what the sweep of the skirt is. Such a hem may distort the drape and interfere with the silhouette.

Make sure your fabric has time to hang out before finalizing the hem—overnight is sufficient for most fabrics. Flared, circular, or gored skirts; garments made of crepe, chiffon, knits, and stretch fabrics; and garments cut on the bias need 24 hours to allow any bias seams or areas to hang out. Otherwise, you may have a sagging, uneven finished hem.

Before finalizing your hem, experiment with its length with everything in place. Inserting pins at right angles to the raw hem edge, pin the hem at different lengths until you find one that is right for you, the design, and your accessories. Check the length of a straight fitted skirt while sitting too.

Use pins, chalk, or a combination of these; adjust the skirt marker to your needs. For most accuracy, have someone else mark your hem, moving around you while you stand still. Place pins every 3″ for straight skirts and every 2″ for flared skirts.

After the hemline has been marked, thread trace it and pin up the hem again; place pins at right angles to the raw hem edge, using pins as needed so the hem falls naturally. The hem should be parallel to the floor, regardless of length.

To finish a hem, refer to The Vogue Sewing Book, pages 321–324; for couture techniques, see pages 367–368; for pressing, see page 331.

Plaids and stripes can be a problem when marking a hem—your eye will immediately focus on a predominant stripe in the plaid or a horizontal stripe that is a trifle off near the hemline. Correct the hem gradually until it is visually straight. However, there are some styles—such as an A-line silhouette—when the visual problems of the hem cannot be corrected optically. The predominant stripe in the plaid or the horizontal stripe seems to bow across the center of the garment, while chevroning at the side seams.

Bias-cut garments or circular skirts need to be handled with care once you have established the appropriate length. Over-handling can cause ripples in the hem area that can never be eliminated. Be careful not to stretch or distort the fabric while finishing the hem—this may undo all of your previous careful planning.

Pleats in the hem may need some special attention so the under folds are not visible. Raise the inner pleat crease the amount needed, tapering each layer of the inner fold to the foldline or roll line and the placement line.

Lining hems are easy to complete after fitting the lining (see pages 87–88) and sewing it in place permanently. Place the garment on your dress form or on a padded hanger attached to a wire suspended from the ceiling—you must be able to work around the garment.

With the garment in position, fasten closure edges smoothly, allowing the lining to drape naturally inside the garment. From the outside, pin lining to the garment 4″–8″ above the hem; place the pins at right angles at 2″–3″ intervals. Do the same for sleeves or pants legs. Choose an appropriate method and finish the hem (see pages 355–356 of The Vogue Sewing Book for the attached lining hem method and the free-hanging method).

Knits do not usually offer trouble when marking the hem, but heavy, stable knits may need special construction. If ridges or bubbles form on the outside of the hem area, you can usually add interfacing even though the garment has not been underlined. Cut your hem interfacing about 1½″ wider than the hem allowance and attach it as you normally would. Since the interfacing will be exposed, you might want to line your stable knit garment.

Pants hems should be of a length which just touches the instep without causing breaks or wrinkles across the front crease. The pants should cover the ankle bone. If this results in an extremely shaped hem and your fabric is crisp or tightly woven, it may be easier to make a faced hem.

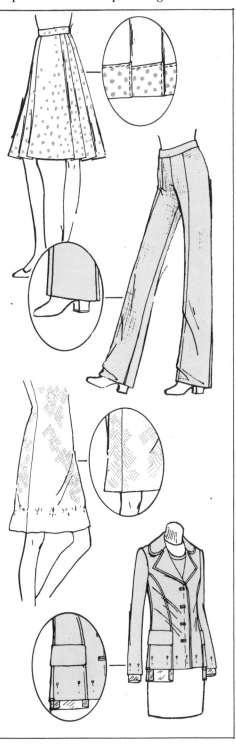

Fitting for Impeccable Details

How often does the diligent and conscientious seamstress fall short of her fashion mark by losing her zest and exuberance as she approaches those small fashion and fitting details? She mistakenly feels that sewing on a button is hardly a couture touch, when in fact, buttons do have great impact on maintaining fit and hang. Snaps, hooks and eyes, lingerie straps, waistline stays, French tacks, and weights will help to ensure perfect fit, wearability, and comfort. Linings, underlinings, and bound buttonholes are couture touches that have previously been built into or attached to your garment; they are details that make your garment truly special. Inside trims can be simply decorative, but more often than not they can be used as a special construction technique, like lace on a hem that decorates as well as clean finishes a raw edge. The woman who sews has this final opportunity to add those extra touches that supplement the fit and enjoyment of her garment, and it is her option to be as lavish with these extras as her taste and energy will permit.

When you have sewn on your buttons, check to see that their weight does not distort the fit of the garment by causing gaping or pulling. Make sure the button is placed directly beneath the buttonhole, or it will cause pulling and wrinkling. Add a thread shank to a sew-through button to maintain smooth fit in the closure area. The careful positioning of a snap or a hook and eye will improve the fit of the garment. A snap or hook and eye at the corner of a neckline, inside the underlap of a wrap dress, or at the tip of a fabric belt will add extra vitality to your fashion. The Vogue Sewing Book contains information on covering snaps and hooks and eyes.

Maintaining the fit of a double-breasted garment may require that snaps be sewn to the underlap so your fabric is supported. Otherwise, it will collapse underneath, causing unsightly wrinkles which show from the outside. To find the correct position for your snaps or hooks and eyes, button your garment, placing underlap in position so it falls smoothly and its hem is slightly shorter than garment hem. Pin underlap in position; unbutton your garment, leaving the pin in place until you have marked the position of the snap or hook on underlap and on the inside of garment overlap to which it will be secured.

When fitting a convertible neckline, plan to place a thread loop and a tiny button at the neckline so the closure will be inconspicuous when the neckline is worn open. Do not hesitate to use a thread loop with a hook rather than the traditional hook and eye, if you find that it will be more compatible with your fashion fabric.

To assure the impact of a well-fitting garment, make lingerie straps to keep your bra straps from slipping over your shoulders. Use snaps and thread chains, seam binding, or lace. The Vogue Sewing Book provides information on how to make these.

Sometimes a cowl neckline, a skirt, or the hemline of a jacket needs weights to maintain the hang of the fabric. Chain weights sewn just above the hemline of a jacket improve the drape of your garment. There are also flat circular weights and lead weight strips. Covering a flat circular weight with a bit of your fashion fabric provides a luxurious touch. If your fabric is bulky, use your lining fabric to cover the weight, then fasten it in place with a French tack. French tacks can also be used most effectively on collars or at the corners of flaps to keep them in the correct position.

When fitting dresses with very full skirts, skirts that are heavier than the bodices, and princess-line or sheath dresses, you will want to add a waist stay of grosgrain ribbon. This will support the weight of the skirt, keep the waist securely in place, and avoid distortion of the fit of the bodice.

Add hanger straps at the waistline of your garment to preserve its fit and shape when it is not being worn. Make a loop of ribbon seam binding and tack it to the waist. The loops should slip on and off the hanger easily. In knitted dresses, you may want to add long loops of ribbon seam binding at the waistline so that when placed over the hanger, they will support the weight of the skirt portion of the dress.

WITHOUT STAY   WITH STAY

A superbly fitted garment deserves to be as beautiful on the inside as it is on the outside. A tiny edge of lace or soutache braid whipstitched at the seamline of a lining or facing can add another fashion dimension to your garment. As long as your inside trim creates no ridges or lumps, let your imagination roam—consider trimming the inside of your garment with narrow braid or ribbon. Trim and cover a zipper tape with lace. To differentiate between the back and front of pants or skirts—especially when the waist is elasticized—sew an "X" with contrasting buttonhole twist on the inside of the back waist.

Touch-up and Finale

A thoughtful touch-up pressing ensures lasting perfect fit in your fashion garment. Lavish attention on small wrinkles and tiny puckers whose disappearance will further enhance your masterpiece. If you have faithfully pressed during all phases of construction, this touch-up will be needed only to refine your fashion.

This last pressing cannot be expected to resolve fitting problems or the effects of neglectful pressing throughout construction. Pressing at this point is actually minimal, but may well be crucial to the precise fit and flawless finished appearance of your garment.

Use all the pressing tools at your disposal. Improvise if you do not have every special tool. Often one tool can serve the function of another if used imaginatively. If you have a dress form, it can pay special dividends; using it to spot-steam the roll of a collar and lapel, patch pocket, or sleeve cap will bring your fitting efforts to a professional and rewarding end. To substitute for a dress form, suspend a heavy, padded wooden hanger by wire from a door frame. Filling out your sleeve cap with wadded tissue paper will also help professionalize your touchup pressing.

Mold and press lovingly to make permanent the fit and shape so carefully built into your garment. Use with inspiration your press mitt, sleeve roll, tailor's ham, brown paper, sleeve board, pounder or clapper, terry cloth or needleboard, point presser, and press cloths of many weights and thicknesses. These items transform your flat ironing board into an assortment of three-dimensional platforms on which you can further mold fit into your fabric. With the aid of a good steam iron—first tested and then set to the appropriate temperature—and your pressing tools, you can turn any garment into a fabric sculpture duplicating your figure. Press with a gentle, but insistent hand, coaxing the contours of your fashion to assume the fit so carefully built into it.

The Vogue Sewing Book (pages 325–331) contains complete pressing information. Touch-up pressing at the culmination of meticulous fitting involves these points:

- ☐ Support fabric by placing a chair under ironing board so the garment will not hang loosely, distorting its fit.
- ☐ If your garment has much fabric—as in a long, full dress or cape—cover the floor with a sheet to prevent soiling.
- ☐ Make sure the ironing board is clean; remove pins and threads.
- ☐ Check the iron sole plate; make sure this is clean and smooth, particularly if your fabric is light-colored or delicate.
- ☐ Adjust the temperature setting properly and test on a sample before pressing. Too much heat can shrivel a synthetic. Test a swatch of lining as well—using an inappropriate lining can cause serious trouble if it reacts to heat and moisture differently from your fashion fabric.
- ☐ All pressing tools should be free of lint, threads, and pins. Make sure that they are readily available near the ironing board.

When touching-up your garment what is generally required is a light hand. Avoid pressing in the outlines of facings, pockets, and seam allowances as these nullify the effect of perfect fit. If you find seams puckering a bit, particularly near a hem, stretch the seams gently as you press, holding the fabric taut with one hand.

When pressing hems, it is your option to strive for a sharp or a soft edge, depending on the garment style and fabric; test both types of edges on a scrap of fabric first. Generally, pleats and vents and hard-faced fabrics require a sharp edge to fall gracefully. Flared styles and knits and soft wools can take a softly pressed edge.

When touching-up collars, pockets, flaps, and welts, pat them gently into place as determined in the last fitting; use a tailor's ham, seam roll, or press mitt. Secure the flap or welt in position with a pin if desired. When touching-up a zipper area, cover it with press cloth. If there are any puckers which distort fit, stretch the zipper area gently as you press. Cover hooks and eyes and snaps when pressing so that impressions do not appear on the outside. Press around buttons, never on them.

You may prefer to have an expert give your garment that last treatment which will guarantee the permanence of your fitting efforts. Locate an excellent tailor or dry cleaner who can press your jackets, pleated skirts, and cuffed pants to perfection.

Your creative role in fitting your fashion garment ends here, and now only maintenance is ahead. Locate a suitable dry cleaner and presser, or consider the method by which it should be laundered. Be prepared to spend a few extra minutes in keeping snaps and hooks and eyes secure, as they are critical to superb fit. Tuck away extra buttons and fabric scraps for the unexpected mishap.

Through all the ups and downs, the challenges and pitfalls, you have emerged victorious . . . the proud creator of a fashion garment that conforms beautifully to your figure, and that harmonizes all the elements of fabric, design, and fit. It is no small thing to have accomplished this in one garment which **you visualized** and strove for, using your skills to the fullest. Now you can rest, assured that the fitting techniques you have learned will never fail you, but will grow and improve with use.

Fitting Resolutions in Terms of Fashion

Fitting is a process that is both challenging and fun—and has the supreme plus of providing tremendous satisfaction when it transforms your Vogue Pattern and fabric ideal into a fashion that is your own like no other has ever been. The manner in which all representative styles can be made to conform perfectly to your figure has been established in the text of this book. But, because fashion sewing—particularly in the vein of the Haute Couture—certainly involves more than these representative styles, we have collected a group of Vogue Patterns whose design lines are typical of those which might be chosen to flatter a particular figure, yet which seem rather complex to alter. We have interpreted these designs in fabrics which you might select, and altered the patterns to fit women whose figure flaws are most frequently shared by others. Each fashion on the following pages presents an unresolved fitting problem, the single or multiple alteration it requires, and—as a *proof* of the personal fitting theories presented throughout this book—the perfect fit which is achieved. Analyze them in light of you and your sewing —and give into the inspiration offered by great fashion, fabric, and fit.

GRAPHS BY NEAL BARR   FABRICS COURTESY OF ELEGANCE INTERNATIONAL

If you have a high bust, and bust shaping in clothes is incorrectly positioned...

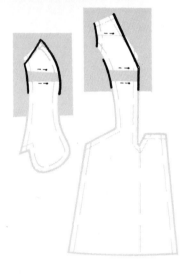

Because the bust shaping built into the garment is too low for the apex of the bust, there are wrinkles of excess fabric and pulling over the apex. An adaptation of the alteration of the classic princess style on page 158 has been used to align the curves of the pattern with those of the body. This alteration concerns only the front pattern pieces.

If you have a large bust cup, and clothes are too tight in this area...

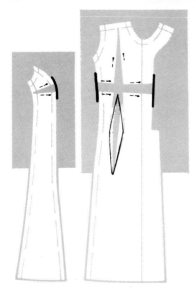

In addition to being tight in the bust area, the neckline of the dress pulls and gapes because there is not enough fabric to mold smoothly over body contours. To remedy this by providing adequate girth in the bosom area of the pattern, we have adapted the alteration of the classic princess style on page 156. Note that only the front pattern pieces require alteration.

If you have bulging thighs, and clothes bind below your hips...

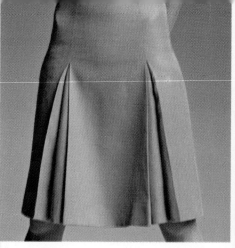

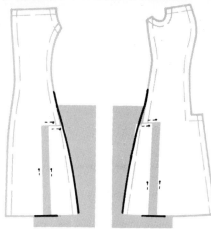

Due to the protrusion of the thighs just below the full hipline, the pleats of the dress spread, and its side seams are distorted. Wrinkles and creases of strain are evident in the crisp fabric. The alteration for thigh bulge (page 172) has been used to relieve the tightness, enable the pleats to hang straight, and provide adequate fabric to fit body contours. Equal changes are made on both front and back pattern pieces.

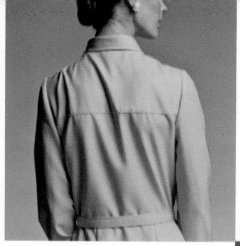

If you have a narrow erect back, and clothes have deep folds here...

A dress which combines a crisp fabric and yoke seaming has pronounced vertical wrinkles and bubbling in the rigid garment back because it is too wide and long for the body. To remove excess width, the back pattern pieces only have been slashed and lapped; clipping the shoulder seam allowance enables the pattern to lie flat. This is simply an adaptation of the alteration used for styles which have back darts (page 165). The center back length has been decreased to accommodate the erect back.

If you have a short crotch length and large abdomen, and pants pull here...

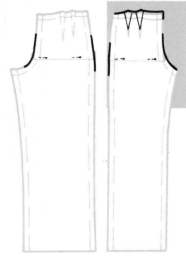

The fullness of body curves sometimes requires greater length along the center front than has been built into the pattern. Wrinkles and pulling are evident across the upper legs, and the curve of the crotch seam does not correspond to that of the body. In resolving these problems, the crotch length has been shortened (page 119), on both front and back pattern pieces and the alteration for a large abdomen (page 175) has been made on the front pattern piece.

If you have large buttocks, and clothes strain across your derrière...

Even though the hip circumference of the pattern is adequate, there is insufficient fabric to mold smoothly over body contours. Pulling over the buttocks and at the inseams, and wrinkles of strain around these areas can be eliminated by increasing the length of the back and the inseam. This alteration can be found on page 180; note that only the back pattern piece requires change.

If you have narrow uneven shoulders, and clothes wrinkle in this area...

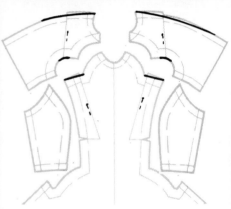

Often a figure which has narrow shoulders also has one which slopes, resulting in a slightly asymmetrical appearance. In this dress there is excess fabric in both raglan sleeves, but they do not react to the body in the same way. To eradicate bubbles and wrinkles, the alteration for narrow shoulders (page 140) has been employed; also the left half of the bodice pattern has been shortened to remove the excess fabric between the shoulder and bust.

BOOK II

Fashion Dimensions on the Level

Adjusting
to a
Better Fit

Pattern **adjustments** involve changing the pattern tissue to allow for simple length and circumference variations between you and the standard body measurements on which the pattern has been based. Adjustments are neither difficult nor time-consuming; once you have learned how to make any necessary adjustments, many subsequent fitting problems can be quickly resolved. You will be able to apply the adjustment needed on a bodice, for example, to every bodice you sew, whether a dress, jacket, vest, or jumpsuit. Pattern **alterations,** which resolve more localized and asymmetrical figure problems, are thoroughly covered in Book III.

Flat pattern adjustments are the easiest changes to make. Adjustments are made on the **flat pattern tissue,** and each pattern piece must remain flat after the changes have been made. Later, alterations will be transferred to this same pattern. The importance of adjusting and altering your pattern is primary. Once you have cut into your fashion fabric, you cannot make any major changes. It would truly be a tragedy if beautiful fashion fabric were cut too small or too large; attempts to adjust and alter after the fact can ruin the lines of a dress and distort wearing ease. The resulting disaster would represent a waste of time, money, and fabric.

Self-analysis

From taking your own measurements and from experience with ill-fitting garments, you will be able to pick out which adjustments are needed. Use the measuring instructions on pages 22–23 for an accurate comparison of your body with standard measurements. Length adjustments adapt the vertical length of the pattern to your body needs; circumference adjustments assist you in keeping the wearing ease of your pattern intact so your garment will drape over your curves attractively. After you have realized a need for flat pattern adjustments, turn to pages 100–101 where you will find quick and easy methods for making your changes.

Your Ups and Downs

Even if your circumference proportions are good, you may still find yourself with figure variations—you may be long-waisted and short-hipped, or short-waisted and long-hipped. Garments you have purchased or made in the past will have demonstrated your particular problem, as will a comparison of your measurements with the standard pattern measurements. A dress that is too short-waisted will have a sagging hipline and perhaps be too tight where it lies above the natural waistline. A dress that is too long-waisted will wrinkle and bunch above the waistline. An easily corrected fitting problem, shortening or lengthening your pattern is crucial.

On pants, for example, if the crotch pulls downward or is baggy, you have another length problem. When an accurate crotch measurement has been compared to the pattern and suitably adjusted, comfort and style ease plus wearing ease will be maintained in the pattern. Any further fitting will be readily evident in your muslin shell. Many women also need length adjustments in pants legs between the crotch line and knee, and the knee and hem to accommodate individual leg length.

On skirts, the hipline is often a problem — it may ride too low on your hips, distorting the lines of the skirt, or it may cause the waistline to reach up to the midriff, again affecting design lines. Vogue Patterns has established the full hip 9″ below the waist for Misses' and Women's, and 7″ below the waist for Miss Petite and Half-Size. If skirts and pants patterns are purchased by hip measurement, only a length adjustment should be needed, as circumference has been accommodated. However, since many women are not statistically proportioned, length and circumference adjustments may be required in patterns not purchased by hip measurement alone.

Round-about You

When a woman's proportions are dissimilar, her garment will usually need circumference adjustments. When these adjustments have been made on the pattern tissue and cut into the lines of the garment, the fit will flatter and help to hide the imperfect proportions of the waist and hips. Waist and hip areas that are too small, for example, will pull and be tight below the bust; when too large, they will hang loosely and sag below the bustline. An excessively tight waist alone will bind, feeling uncomfortable and looking worse. With tight hip fit, the skirt has a tendency to ride up and eradicate wearing ease. An excessively large waist alone will hang loosely and ruin style lines; the same is true when there is extra fabric in the hip area.

Circumference adjustments in waist and hips, necessary in all garments if your measurements are not "standard," are sometimes unnecessary in skirt or pants patterns purchased by waist or hip measurements. Adjustments should be completed in the pattern tissue before cutting and constructing the muslin fitting shell or fashion garment. The adjusted muslin fitting shell may reveal other flaws which can be corrected by pattern alterations. Rely on your accurate measurements and your past experiences with ill-fitting garments to adjust your pattern and to make your wardrobe individually yours.

Specialties of the House

Vogue Patterns endeavors to bring you the best in fashion from the haute couture — these designs are master-works of subtle construction. Intricate style lines, curved seams, geometric seams, asymmetrical seams, and French darts are unique shapes which cannot be simply adjusted when shortening or lengthening. Such seaming is more than a means to hold a dress together — it is what makes that particular dress the individualized fashion it is. When carefully adjusted, these patterns will both compliment you and add immensely to the character of your wardrobe.

To Adjust With Accuracy

Always make all necessary adjustments on your pattern pieces *before cutting* anything—whether for your fitting muslin or your fashion fabric. The rules presented here are fundamental, and you must interpret them and adapt your specific pattern adjustments accordingly. On Vogue Patterns, the adjustment lines are located within the correct body area or there are other indications of where to adjust the length; adjustments must be made in these areas if the style lines of your fashion pattern are to be maintained. Some designs with complex fashion lines—geometric, curved, or asymmetrical—preclude adjustment; if so, this is stated on the pattern envelope. However, do not hesitate to choose these patterns if the adjustments you require are minor, as we feel that many of our customers will be able to accept the challenge which they present (see pages 122–124).

Throughout Book II wherever pattern pieces are illustrated, *only front pattern pieces are shown. Equal changes are made on front, back, and other related pieces like facings, waistbands, linings, etc.* On pattern pieces, *bold lines* indicate corrected cutting and dart lines. If the *adjustment is localized,* you will be alerted. As a guide in relating adjustments to other basic shapes, you will also find illustrated princess lines, raglan and kimono sleeves, gored and circular skirts, etc. where applicable.

☐ First press all pattern pieces flat with a warm dry iron.
☐ When making *length adjustments,* pin the change in place; then check your accuracy with a ruler along the entire adjustment line before securing the change permanently with tape (use a tape on which you will be able to write).
☐ When making *circumference adjustments,* make sure you have reduced or enlarged the correct amount at the exact spot you need—hip, waist, thigh, etc.
☐ Always keep grainlines and "Place on Fold" lines straight. Check with a transparent ruler to be sure that straight lines are maintained.
☐ Use discretion in making adjustments so your fashion's style lines will not be distorted.
☐ Preserve the wearing ease built into pattern—never use it as part of your adjustment.

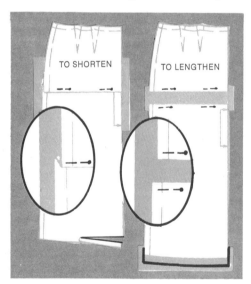

LENGTH ADJUSTMENTS decrease or increase the vertical length of your pattern and may affect the fabric yardage needed. *To shorten the garment area,* crease the pattern along the adjustment lines, folding half the amount of the needed change (when flattened, the fold will be doubled). *To shorten at lower edges,* mark the change, following pattern curves; cut away excess pattern.

To lengthen within the garment area, slash at adjustment lines, place tissue paper beneath slash, and spread cut edges as needed. *To lengthen at lower edges,* extend pattern pieces with tissue paper; mark the amount of change, following pattern shape. Draw new cutting lines.

CIRCUMFERENCE ADJUSTMENTS decrease or increase the width of your pattern and may affect fabric yardage. When making circumference adjustments, remember that each major pattern piece (except sleeves) represents one quarter of your body—visualize your figure halved horizontally at the waist and halved vertically at center front and back. Consequently, each bodice or skirt pattern piece must be decreased or increased one quarter of the total adjustment needed.

To reduce the circumference within the garment area more than 1″, slash the pattern as far as necessary so it will lie flat when you lap the edges the amount to be decreased. Clip seam allowance to seamline, or clip hem allowance to hemline so pattern lies flat. Taking in 1″ or less is done by drawing new cutting lines on the pattern.

To enlarge the circumference within the garment area more than 1″, slash the pattern as far as is necessary for the pattern to lie flat. Place tissue paper under the slashed edges and spread the amount needed. Form a pleat in the seam allowance or hem allowance so the pattern will lie flat. Letting out 1″ or less is done by drawing new cutting lines on the pattern.

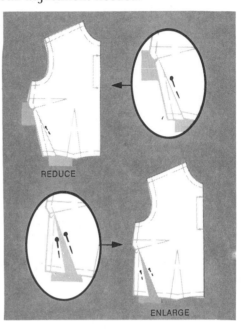

REDUCE

ENLARGE

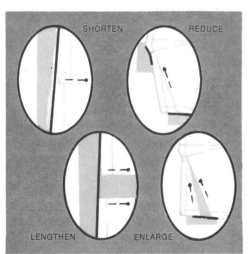

SHORTEN   REDUCE

LENGTHEN   ENLARGE

RE-DRAW INTERRUPTED LINES to achieve smooth construction lines that will not distort the style. Use a felt tip pen or a soft, thick lead pencil so you can see new lines clearly if you must cut out the pattern printed side down. Merely connecting the original lines will not do—you must add to one interrupted line and subtract from the other, re-establishing the smooth contours of your pattern's cutting and stitching lines. Taper new lines to original ones and connect interrupted grainlines. In some cases it may be necessary to extend the pattern edges with tissue paper to re-draw the cutting lines.

The rules and guidelines which are outlined on this and the previous page should be followed for every adjustment your body requires to achieve a finished garment in the grand manner. Once you have mastered these simple procedures, you will find that adjustments are easy.

Length Adjustments

In lengthening and/or shortening your fashion pattern to align it with the vertical proportions of your figure, you create a pattern that is unique — there may be no other person with your particular combination of dimensions.

Shortening Pattern Pieces

Adjustment lines are positioned to create a minimum of style distortion. Review pages 100–101 if you need the illustrated procedures clarified. Your measurements (see pages 22–23) show the amount each area must be shortened.

BODICE LENGTH   SLEEVE LENGTH   SKIRT LENGTH TO FULL HIPLINE

BODICE: Shorten as indicated. For an A-line or princess style whose bodice is cut-in-one with the skirt, this adjustment is critical to the fit of your fashion garment. Make this same adjustment in blouses, jackets, coats, vests, etc.

SLEEVE: For a fitted or raglan sleeve, shorten along either or both sets of adjustment lines (depending on your arm measurements). Fuller sleeves such as bell, shirt, or kimono usually have just one set of adjustment lines.

FULL HIPLINE: To raise the full hipline, make adjustment just above the indicated hipline. Use your basic fitted garment pattern as a guide to make this change on all your fashion patterns.

SKIRT: Even if the hipline has been raised, your skirt may still need to be shortened. Shorten most gored or circular skirts at the lower edge. If your skirt has a band, pleated section, or other form of decorative detailing at the lower edge, use the adjustment line above the seamline.

BACK WAIST LENGTH (base of neck to waist): This may be the *only* length adjustment needed; do not confuse it with alterations for figure flaws in Book III. Shorten fitted and A-line styles at the center back, tapering to side seam. For a princess style, adjust all back pieces.

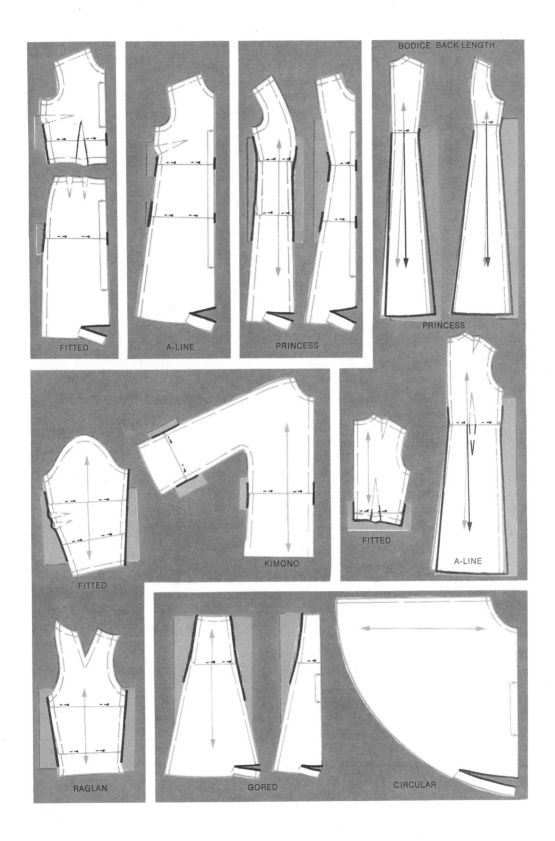

FITTED

A-LINE

PRINCESS

BODICE BACK LENGTH

PRINCESS

FITTED

KIMONO

FITTED

A-LINE

RAGLAN

GORED

CIRCULAR

Lengthening Pattern Pieces

Adjustment lines are carefully situated to create a minimum of style distortion. Review the rules on pages 100—101 for further clarification of the illustrated procedures. Your measurements, when correctly taken as directed on pages 22–23, will show how much each pattern piece must be lengthened.

BODICE: Lengthen separate bodice pieces as illustrated. For an A-line or princess style whose bodice is cut-in-one with the skirt, this adjustment is extremely important. Otherwise, you may be unable to fit the fashion garment satisfactorily. Make this adjustment in blouses, jackets, coats, vests, etc.

SLEEVE: Lengthen fitted or raglan sleeves along either or both sets of adjustment lines, depending on which part of your arm requires greater length. Sleeves that are less fitted—like bell, shirt, or kimono styles—usually have only one set of adjustment lines where any changes will least affect design lines.

FULL HIPLINE: To lower the full hipline, make adjustment just above the indicated hipline. Then use your basic fitted garment pattern as a guide to make this adjustment on all your fashion patterns.

SKIRT: Although the hipline has been lowered, the skirt may still need to be lengthened. Practically all gored and circular skirts should be lengthened at the lower edge. However, if your skirt is stylized and has a band, pleated section, etc. at the lower edge, you will find an adjustment line above the seamline so the sweep of the skirt will not be changed.

BODICE BACK LENGTH: This adjustment is somewhat unusual, since the *only* length deviation is the back measurement from the base of the neck to the waist. It is not to be confused with figure flaws (an erect back, sway back, etc.) which are alterations covered in Book III. Lengthen fitted and A-line styles at center back, tapering to the side seamline. For a princess style, change all back pieces.

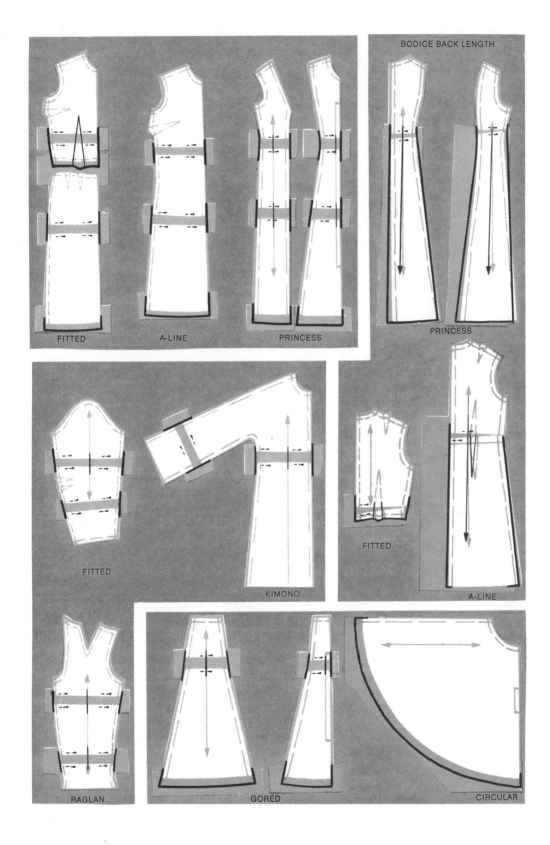

BODICE BACK LENGTH

FITTED

A-LINE

PRINCESS

PRINCESS

FITTED

KIMONO

FITTED

A-LINE

RAGLAN

GORED

CIRCULAR

Circumference Adjustments

For a garment to lie smoothly over your body contours, the circumferences of both must be in agreement. It is often necessary to adjust the circumference of various areas of a pattern to proportion it like your body, building your curves into the pattern before cutting out the fabric. The bust area is not discussed here, since patterns are purchased by bust measurement. In Book III you will learn how to alter the bust area, if necessary. Your measurements, when taken as indicated on pages 22 – 23 and compared to the standard body measurements for your pattern size, will show how much each circumference measurement needs to be adjusted. Refer to pages 100 – 101 if you need further explanation of the illustrated procedures.

Reducing Waist and Hips

Circumference reductions for waist and hip fall into two categories: reductions of 1″ or less, and of more than 1″. Reductions must be considered in this way so as not to distort the style lines of the finished garment. Reduce only the amount needed; when doing so, be sure never to take any wearing ease from the waist and hips.

REDUCING WASIT AND HIPS 1″ OR LESS: Mark ¼ of the amount to be reduced at the waist and hipline along the side seam. Pin in the bust dart. Draw new cutting lines, tapering from waist to bustline. Remove pins, and then complete the tapered line at the dart.

TOO LOOSE   CORRECT

For *princess* and *A-line* styles, adjust the side seams only. To reduce skirt shapes like *gored, slim gathered,* or a *less-than-full circular* skirt 1″ or less, mark ¼ of the needed reduction along the side seam. For a *full circular* skirt, reduce ¼ of the amount needed at both center foldline and seamline.

REDUCING WAIST AND HIPS MORE THAN 1″: For a style with a *waist seam,* slash the bodice and skirt as shown; do not disturb the grainline. Lap slashed edges ¼ of the amount needed. Re-draw cutting lines.

For a *princess* style, divide amount to be reduced by number of seams (excluding center front or back); halve this figure. Mark the amount needed and draw new cutting lines, tapering from waist to bust and full hip to hem.

A-line styles *should not* be reduced more than 1″, as style lines will be distorted. For *a gored, slim gathered, or less-than-full circular* skirt more than 1″, divide the reduction by the number of seams; halve this figure for each seam edge reduction. For a *full circular* skirt, reduce ¼ of the amount needed at centers.

WAISTBAND: Reduce waistband for a separate skirt the full amount, making half the adjustment at center front and back or at side seam markings.

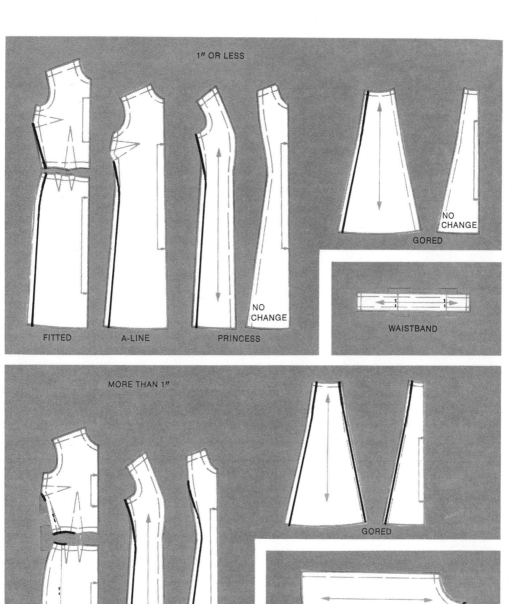

1″ OR LESS

FITTED

A-LINE

PRINCESS

NO CHANGE

GORED

NO CHANGE

WAISTBAND

MORE THAN 1″

FITTED

PRINCESS

GORED

CIRCULAR

Enlarging Waist and Hips

Enlarging the circumference of the waist and hips is necessary to proportion fashions for women who have a small bust and large waist and hips.

TOO TIGHT   CORRECT

ENLARGING WAIST AND HIPS 1″ OR LESS: Add tissue paper to the side seams. For styles with a *waist seam,* mark ¼ of the amount needed at bodice and skirt waist and skirt full hip; pin bust dart. On the bodice, taper new cutting lines from waist to bust. Un-pin bust dart, finish cutting lines, and press tissue. Connect skirt markings, and taper new cutting lines from hip to lower edge.

For A-line and princess styles, mark ¼ of the amount to be enlarged at the waist and hips. Pin the bust dart. Taper new cutting lines from waist to bust and hip to lower edge. Un-pin the dart, finish cutting lines, and press tissue.

Enlarge *gored, slim gathered, or semi-circular* skirts similarly. For a *full circular skirt,* shift center foldline or seamline out ¼ of amount (not shown).

ENLARGING WAIST AND HIPS MORE THAN 1″: On a style with a waist seam, slash the bodice and skirt as shown. Avoid disturbing the grainline. Place tissue paper under the slash and spread the pattern ¼ of the amount needed; pin. Check the adjustment and fasten with tape. Form a small pleat in the bodice seam allowance or skirt hem allowance to make the pattern lie flat. Re-draw all broken cutting lines.

For an A-line style, slash at the waist, then down through skirt. Place tissue paper under slash and spread ¼ of amount needed. Pin, check, and tape. Draw new cutting lines, tapering to the bust. A small pleat may form in the hem allowance.

For a princess style, the method of adjustment to use depends on the fullness of your figure. If you are full-busted and want to retain the curves in the side front seams, enlarge by slashing as shown at the side seams only; slash in at the waistline, then upward, far enough to keep the pattern flat. Place tissue paper under the slash and side seam. Spread pattern edges ¼ of the amount needed; a small pleat may form in the armhole seam allowance. Pin, check, and tape. Draw new cutting lines.

For a smaller-busted figure, the curves can be adjusted at each seam; follow the procedure for enlarging waist and hips 1″ or less.

To enlarge other skirt shapes—like *slim gathered or semi-circular*—slash and enlarge as for the fitted skirt. Mark ¼ of the amount needed and draw new cutting lines. For a gored skirt, divide the amount needed by the number of seams; halve this figure and add to each seam edge, inserting tissue paper, marking, and re-drawing cutting lines. On a full circular skirt, add tissue to center foldline or seamline, mark ¼ of needed amount, and draw a new foldline or cutting line (not shown).

WAISTBAND: Enlarge the waistband of a separate skirt the full amount, making half the adjustment at center front and back or at side seam markings.

1″ OR LESS

NO
CHANGE

GORED

SLIM GATHERED

NO
CHANGE

FITTED   A-LINE   PRINCESS

MORE THAN 1″

SLIM GATHERED

NO
CHANGE

FITTED   A-LINE   PRINCESS

GORED

Reducing Waist Without Changing Hips

If you have a slender waistline yet proportionate bust and hips, garments will collapse at your waist giving an unkempt, haphazard look. It will therefore be necessary to reduce the waist without changing the hip circumference — a perfectly fitting waist always compliments you and your sewing ability.

TOO LOOSE | CORRECT

On the bodice and skirt side seam of a garment with a *waist seam*, mark ¼ of the amount needed to be reduced. Draw new cutting lines, tapering from waist to just below the bust on the bodice, and from waist to just above the full hipline on the skirt; the hip circumference is not reduced.

To reduce the waist of an *A-line* garment, mark ¼ of the amount needed at the waist indication. Draw new cutting lines, tapering from waist to near the bust dart, and from the waist to just above the full hipline. The line should not be tapered to the full hipline as doing so would reduce your pattern's hip measurement.

To reduce the waist of a *princess* style garment, there are two advance considerations. If you have a full figure, you can safely reduce the waist at the side front and side back seams as well as at the side seams. Divide the amount of reduction by the number of seams; halve this number for the reduction to be made at each seam edge. Mark the amount and draw new cutting lines, tapering from waist to just under the bust, and from waist to just above the full hip, since you do not want to disturb the bust and hip proportions of your pattern.

Or, if you are on the small side, you can make waist reductions in a princess style only at the side seams. To do this, mark ¼ of the amount needed at the waist indication. Draw in new cutting lines, tapering from the waist to just under the bust and from the waist to just above the full hip.

On a *gored* skirt, make the waist reduction at the side seams for a smaller figure; mark ¼ of the amount needed. Draw new cutting lines, tapering from waist to just above the full hipline. Or, for a fuller figure, divide the amount of change by the number of seams as explained above for princess styles.

For a *full circular* skirt, place tissue paper above the waist edge and draw in a new waist seamline, reducing ¼ of the amount needed; follow the curves of the pattern. Then draw new cutting lines and foldlines as indicated on these pattern pieces. On a skirt less-than-full circular which has no hip shaping, the waist reduction is done in the same manner.

WAISTBAND: Adjust a waistband to correspond to the skirt by reducing it the full amount needed. Add one half of the amount of the change at the center front. Add the other half of this amount at the center back or at the side seam markings so all your symbols will match those on the skirt.

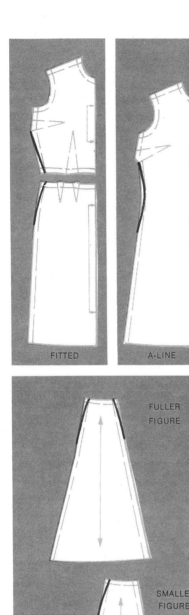

FITTED

A-LINE

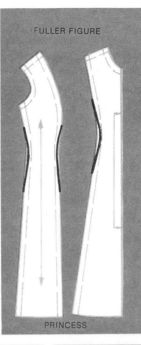

FULLER FIGURE

PRINCESS

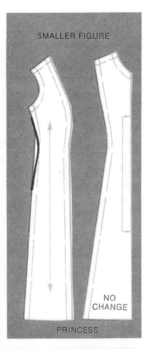

SMALLER FIGURE

NO CHANGE

PRINCESS

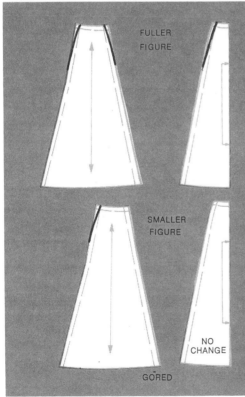

FULLER FIGURE

SMALLER FIGURE

NO CHANGE

GORED

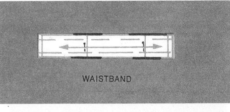

WAISTBAND

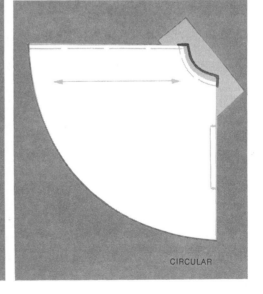

CIRCULAR

Enlarging Waist Without Changing Hips

TOO TIGHT   CORRECT

The woman with a fuller waistline in proportion to her bust and hips is not in possession of a figure flaw—rather it is one of an endless variety of figure types. To avoid making this adjustment not only ruins the look of the garment but also causes pinching and restricts movement. Do not expect to use the built-in wearing ease to accommodate a larger waistline. It will be necessary to enlarge the waist without affecting the hip circumference. After you have taken your measurements as indicated on pages 22–23, you will be able to determine how much of an increase you need. A well-fitted waistline can then be adapted from your basic fitted pattern to all of your subsequent fashion patterns. In doing so you will achieve garments that are truly and perfectly yours.

To a garment with a *waist seam,* add tissue paper to the side seams of the bodice and skirt. Mark ¼ of the amount needed to be enlarged at the waistline. Draw new cutting lines, tapering from the waist to just under the bust on the bodice, and from the waist to just above the full hip on the skirt. Do not allow the new lines to reach the bust dart or the hipline, because the bust and hip measurements should not be disturbed.

For an *A-line* garment, add tissue paper to the side seam. Mark ¼ of the amount needed at the waist and draw new cutting lines; taper from the waist to just under the bust dart, and from the waist to just above the full hipline. This prevents disturbing bust and hip measurements.

To enlarge the waist of a *princess* style, take figure proportions into account. For a smaller figure, the waist may be enlarged at the side seams only. To do this, add tissue paper to the side seam. Mark ¼ of the amount needed to be enlarged and draw in new cutting lines, tapering from the waist to just under the bust and from the waist to just above the full hip, so the hip and bust measurements of your pattern remain the same.

To make this adjustment for a fuller figure, divide the amount needed by the number of seams; halve this figure for the amount of change that will be needed at each seam edge. Do not add to center front or back seams. Then increase the waist as previously explained.

For a *gored* skirt, enlarge the waist at the side seams as explained above for princess style garments. For a *full circular* skirt, draw a new waist seamline ¼ of the amount needed below the existing waist edge; follow the curve of the pattern so that the style line is maintained. Then draw a new cutting line. On a *less-than-full circular* skirt which has no hip shaping, the waist can be increased in a manner similar to that explained above.

WAISTBAND: Enlarge the waistband of a separate skirt the full amount, making half the adjustment at center front and back or at the side seam markings.

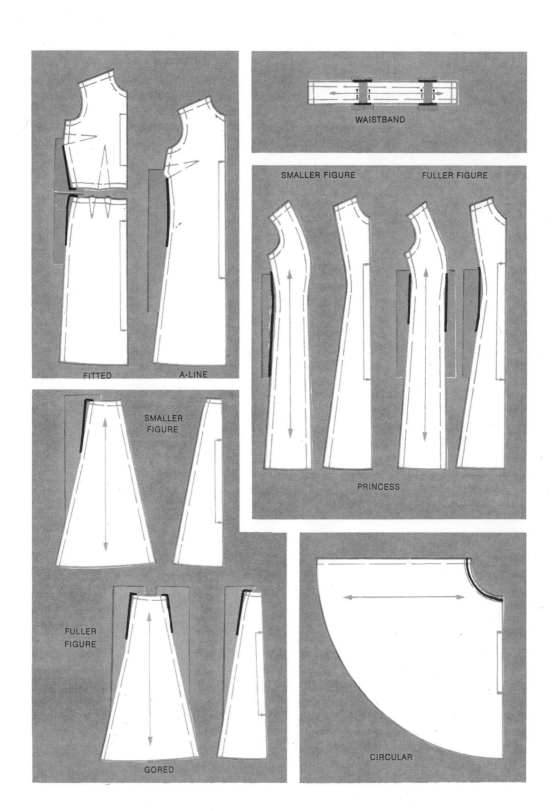

WAISTBAND

SMALLER FIGURE

FULLER FIGURE

FITTED

A-LINE

PRINCESS

SMALLER
FIGURE

FULLER
FIGURE

GORED

CIRCULAR

Reducing Hips Without Changing Waist

TOO LOOSE   CORRECT

Patterns purchased by bust measurement may not fit smoothly across the hips and must be adjusted if the skirt section is not to be distorted. A smooth hip fit draws attention away from hips that are disproportionately small, thus bringing the figure back into proportion visually.

A garment that hangs loosely over the hip area while fitting perfectly in the bust and waist area is *not* a fitted garment; the pattern must be adjusted. By comparing your personal measurements to those of the pattern, you will arrive at the amount of hip adjustment you need. Instructions given here are for reducing hip circumference by 2″ or less. For a reduction of more than 2″, it is best to combine two pattern sizes (see pages 128–129 for these instructions).

Review the rules on pages 100–101 if you feel you need more explanation of the methods and illustrations used here.

For a fitted style with a ***waist seam,*** mark ¼ of the amount needed to be reduced at the full hip indication. Draw new cutting lines, tapering from the full hip to just below the waist. From the hipline to the lower edge keep the amount even. Apply this adjustment to all hip-fitted skirts.

On an ***A-line*** style, the hip should not be reduced more than 1″ as the style lines of your fashion may be distorted or destroyed. To reduce 1″ or less, mark ¼ of the amount needed to be reduced at the full hipline. Draw new seam and cutting lines, tapering from the full hipline to just below waist. From the hipline to the hem, keep the adjustment even, taking from the lower edge the same amount subtracted from the full hipline.

To reduce a ***princess*** style 1″ or less, mark ¼ of the total adjustment necessary at the full hipline at the side seam. Draw new cutting lines, tapering from the hipline to just below the waist indication on the pattern. From the hipline to the hem, keep the amount to be reduced equal in width. Reduce the hem circumference the same amount as the hipline was reduced.

For a reduction of up to 2″ on a princess style, divide the amount to be reduced by the number of seams, excluding the center front and center back seams. Halve this figure in order to find the appropriate amount needed to be reduced at each seam edge. Mark this amount at the full hipline. Draw new cutting lines, tapering from the hipline to just under the waist. Keep the amount to be reduced equal from the hipline to the lower edge of the pattern.

For a ***gored*** skirt, mark ¼ of the total amount to be adjusted at the hipline at the side seam. Draw new cutting lines, tapering from the hipline to just below the waist. Maintain the uniformity of the reduction from the hipline to the lower edge. Other special skirt shapes—like gathered or circular styles—will need no adjustments in the hip area of the pattern.

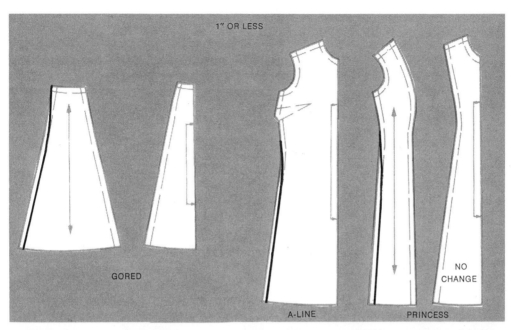

1" OR LESS

GORED

A-LINE

PRINCESS

NO CHANGE

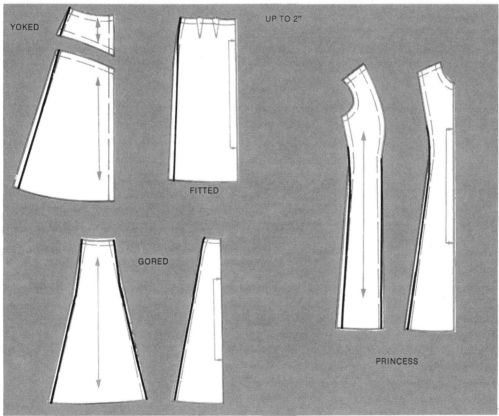

YOKED

UP TO 2"

FITTED

GORED

PRINCESS

115

Enlarging Hips Without Changing Waist

Large hips are a common figure problem among women. Hip fit that covers your contours and does not pull or ride up can de-emphasize large hips. Never use wearing ease to accommodate large hips, as this will distort both style and fit.

TOO TIGHT   CORRECT

ENLARGING HIPS 2″ OR LESS: For a *waist seam* style or *hip-fitted* skirt, add tissue paper to the side edges. Mark ¼ of the amount needed to enlarge at the full hipline. Draw new cutting lines, tapering from the waist to the hipline, and keeping the enlargement even from the hipline to the lower edge. Make the same adjustment when enlarging an *A-line* or *princess* style garment.

To enlarge a *gored* or *slim gathered* skirt 2″ or less, follow the adjustment for a waist seam style, tapering from the waist to the hipline.

For other skirt shapes with a natural waist seam —like a circular skirt—no hip adjustment is needed. However if it will be joined to the garment with a hip seam, enlarge it as you would a waist, page 112.

ENLARGING HIPS MORE THAN 2″: To enlarge a *waist seam* style more than 2″, slash the skirt parallel to the grainline, as shown. Place tissue paper under the slash, and spread the pattern ¼ of the amount needed; pin. Check the adjustment and fasten with tape. Draw in new cutting lines. To remove excess waist circumference, draw an additional dart as shown, or reduce the waist at the side edges as explained on pages 112–113. You can apply this adjustment to any style which involves a skirt fitted in the hip area.

For an *A-line* style, slash pattern parallel to the grainline up to and across the full hipline, as illustrated. Place tissue paper under the slash, spreading the pattern ¼ of the amount needed. Pin, check, and tape. Draw new cutting lines, tapering to bust dart or bust area.

To enlarge a *princess* style 2″ or more, divide the amount needed by the number of seams, excluding center front and center back seams. Halve this figure to get the amount needed at each seam edge. Place tissue paper at the edges. Mark the amount needed at the hipline and lower edges. Draw new cutting lines, tapering from the hip to just below the waist indication.

To enlarge *hip-fitted* skirts, slash as for a fitted skirt and add a dart as indicated. A *circular* skirt with a natural waist seam needs no hip adjustment, while a circular skirt with a hip seam must be enlarged as you would a waist, page 112.

For a *gored* skirt, divide the amount needed to be enlarged by the number of seams, excluding the center front and center back seams. Halve this amount to find the adjustment needed at each seam edge. Add tissue paper to the side edges. Mark the needed amount at the hipline and hem. Then draw new seam and cutting lines, tapering from the waist to the hipline, and keeping the amount even from the hipline to the lower edge of the pattern.

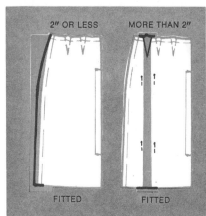

2″ OR LESS — MORE THAN 2″

FITTED — FITTED

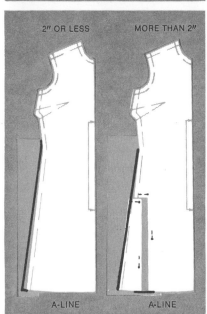

2″ OR LESS — MORE THAN 2″

A-LINE — A-LINE

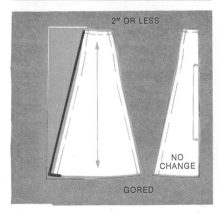

2″ OR LESS

NO CHANGE

GORED

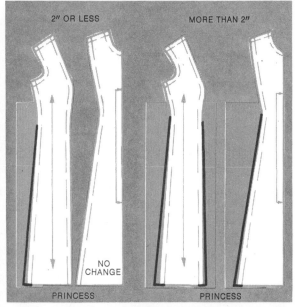

2″ OR LESS — MORE THAN 2″

NO CHANGE

PRINCESS — PRINCESS

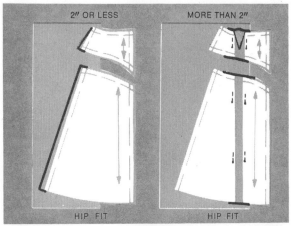

2″ OR LESS — MORE THAN 2″

HIP FIT — HIP FIT

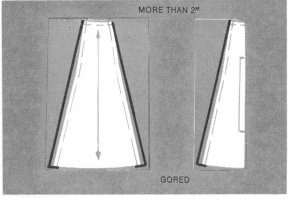

MORE THAN 2″

GORED

Pants Adjustments Resolved

Few fashions can be as flattering and comfortable as a well-fitting pair of pants. Because adjustments are so crucial to the creation of beautiful pants, we have separated them from other pattern adjustments. Your measurements must be built into the pattern before cutting out your pants, or they will never be able to assume the shape you hope to see.

Take the measurements as instructed on pages 22–23. Remember that you will expend less effort and get a better fit if you buy pants patterns by your hip measurement. Compare the pattern's standard body measurements with your own and then adjust the pattern to satisfy your needs.

Fitting pants over figure flaws like a sway back, flat abdomen, etc. will be discussed fully in Book III. Refer to the rules on pages 100–101 if you need further explanation of the methods and illustrations presented.

Length Adjustments

Since your pants may reveal curves you would rather conceal, it is especially important to bring them vertically into proportion with you. This must be done before cutting out your fabric, as incorrect crotch and leg length is impossible to remedy.

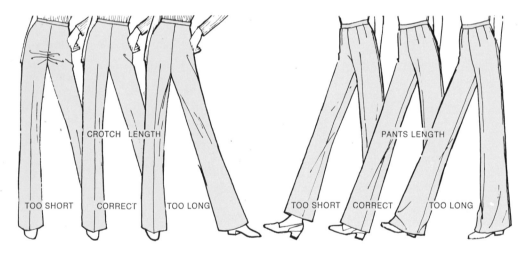

CROTCH LENGTH POSITION: The most important area to be considered when making pants is the pattern crotch length as it compares to your body length. If the crotch is too long, the pants bag in the crotch area; a crotch that is too short binds and pulls. Once you have cut out your fabric no amount of fitting can bring the crotch into the correct position.

Establish a crotch line on your **back pattern piece** if none was given on the pattern. Place a triangle along the grainline and at the lowest point of the seamline or at the widest point of the pattern. Draw a line along the top of the triangle and then extend it across the width of the pattern piece. (See page 119 for illustration.)

CHECK CROTCH LENGTH: To your established crotch measurement add ½″–
¾″ for sitting ease. Then check the pattern length from the waist seamline to the
crotch line, measuring vertically near the side seamline; it must be the exact amount
needed or the pattern must be adjusted. Make the length adjustment along the nearby adjustment lines. **To shorten,** fold out excess length; **to lengthen,** slash and spread
the amount needed over tissue paper. Pin, check adjustment, and secure with tape.
Re-draw seamlines, making a smooth crotch curve. Make an equal adjustment on the
front pattern piece.

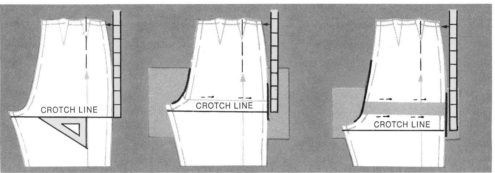

Caution: This adjustment will only bring the crotch curve into the correct position
on your body. Figure flaws—like a large buttock or flat abdomen—that may affect
length in the hip area are discussed in Book III.

OTHER POSITION MARKINGS: Drawing in the other points of your body on
the back pattern piece as they were established by your measurements will help
you a great deal later. To add position
lines, extend the grainline the full length
of the pattern. Using your established
points, measure the distance from the
waist seamline to your *high hip* and make
a dot with a pencil at the location. Place a
triangle on the grainline so the top crosses
the dot and draw a line across the full
width of the pattern. This is the position
marking for your high hip point.

Using the same procedure, indicate your
full hip, thigh, knee, and calf positions on
the side seamline and then transfer the
dots to the side seamline of the front
pattern piece. Draw lines across the pattern as explained above. Establishing these
position markings will greatly facilitate
pants adjustments.

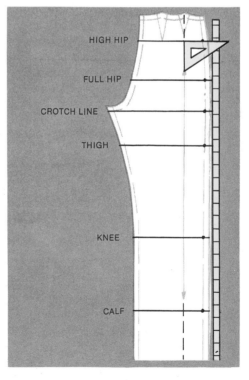

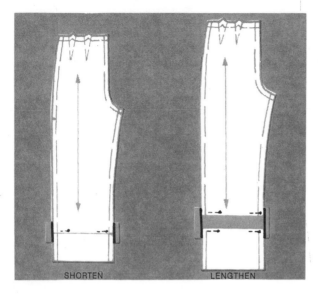

SHORTEN   LENGTHEN

ADJUST PANTS LENGTHS: Determine whether length adjustment should be made at the lower edge or above the knee to preserve style lines. Draw a line as you did to establish the position lines. Use your side length measurement from waist to hemline to determine the need for adjustment.

Shorten by folding out excess along the adjustment line; *lengthen* by slashing and spreading the amount needed over tissue paper. Pin, check adjustment, and secure with tape. Redraw seamlines.

Circumference Adjustments

Even though pants patterns are purchased by hip measurement, some circumference adjustments may be necessary. Pants, which hide very little in the hip area, must lie smoothly to fit well and comfortably. Your measurements, taken accurately and compared with the standard body measurements, will determine both the location and the extent of any adjustment needed.

LEG CIRCUMFERENCE   WAIST CIRCUMFERENCE

TOO TIGHT   CORRECT   TOO LOOSE   TOO TIGHT   CORRECT   TOO LOOSE

WAIST CIRCUMFERENCE: To *decrease,* mark ⅛ of the adjustment needed at each center and side waist edge. Draw new cutting lines, tapering to just above the full hipline. Make corresponding adjustments on the facings or waistband.

To *increase,* add tissue paper at each seam. Mark ⅛ of the amount needed at each side and center seam edge. Draw new cutting lines, tapering to just above the full hipline. Increase facings or waistband the same amount.

For pants styles which have an elasticized waist, no waist adjustment should be necessary.

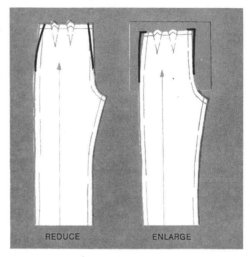

REDUCE   ENLARGE

HIP CIRCUMFERENCE: If you purchased your pattern by hip measurement, no adjustment should be necessary. However, the hip circumference can be altered for figure flaws—large or small buttocks and a protruding or flat abdomen, etc.—that are dealt with in Book III; these are not accommodated by flat pattern adjustments and are personal needs which must be resolved in a pants fitting muslin.

LEG CIRCUMFERENCE: Compare your thigh measurement (plus 1″ wearing ease) to the measurement from seamline to seamline along the established position line on both the back and front pattern pieces. To *reduce,* mark ½ of the amount needed at the inner leg seam, as shown. To *enlarge,* add tissue paper to the inner seam and crotch area and mark ½ of the amount needed. Draw new cutting lines, tapering to the original ones; take care that you maintain the crotch curve.

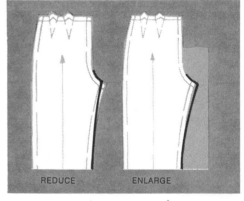

REDUCE   ENLARGE

If you are making tapered, slim-fitted pants, check your knee, calf, and instep measurements, adding at least 1″ wearing ease to each measurement. Measure from seamline to seamline along established position lines on both front and back pattern pieces. Reduce or enlarge circumference as for the thigh (not shown).

Jumpsuit Adjustments

For these practical garments, combine the adjustments techniques of both dresses and pants. For those patterns with separate bodice and pants sections, adjust the bodice and pants as you would any garment with a waist seam, matching darts and seams. Adjust a pattern with a cut-in-one bodice and pants as you would a cut-in-one dress, incorporating the pants adjustments needed.

Special Adjustments Detailed

A challenge for the adventurous woman is mastering flat pattern adjustments which involve unusually shaped pattern pieces or complex seaming details. Combining two patterns, when fashion or the proportions of your figure warrants it is another special technique in adjustments which will be explored.

Intricate Pattern Pieces Adjusted Easily

Vogue Patterns' international designers use complex styling features to create fashions with special dash. Intricate seams and numerous garment sections may cause you to despair at thoughts of fitting when you first remove your pattern from its envelope. Lengthening or shortening these patterns to achieve a better fit may distort the style lines beyond recognition if done by a novice, but the experienced seamstress need not hesitate.

Vogue Patterns are cut in muslin from a sloper in a master size used in making all patterns. These garment shapes are then draped on a dress form made to the standard body measurements for our master size. In draping, the style lines intended by the designer take form; the intricate seaming details are worked exactly into the style lines. When the muslin is approved, the pattern is transferred to heavy paper and is used as a master pattern for this style. A completed garment is made and further refinements take place. If you follow this procedure with your fashion pattern after the adjustments are made, you can make any garment fit. Cut garment portion in muslin; machine baste together. Fit and re-stitch as needed. When fitted to your satisfaction, take the muslin apart and use the pressed seam edges as a guide to transfer corrected style lines to your pattern pieces.

There may be times when your pattern will state "no provisions made for lengthening or shortening." This usually means that the adjustment lines would have to be placed over intricate seaming, and that many people would be unable to make such complicated adjustments. But those who enjoy a challenge should not hesitate to consider customizing these patterns to their proportions.

FRENCH DARTS: This dart shaping usually starts near the waist and extends at an angle upward toward the bust and apex. Its shaping gives you a closer fit since it incorporates a seam with a dart. Careful length adjustments must be made to preserve the dart shaping.

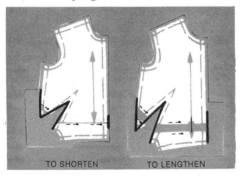

TO SHORTEN   TO LENGTHEN

To shorten, fold out the excess along the adjustment lines. Pin, check adjustment, and secure with tape. Re-draw cutting lines and seamlines as indicated.

To lengthen, slash along the adjustment lines and spread over tissue paper. Pin, check measurement, and secure with tape. Re-draw your correct cutting lines and seamlines.

122

To reduce or enlarge the circumference, most adjustments should be made on the vertical seams where the front joins the back. Otherwise the shapes and style lines may be noticeably and hopelessly distorted. If in doubt, test your garment in muslin before cutting out your fashion fabric.

ASYMMETRICAL SEAMS: It may seem that these will cause little trouble, but such is often not the case. Since the seams are angular, unusual shapes may occur at the cutting line edge when shortening or lengthening. This may distort the seamline if handled incorrectly.

Before making any adjustment on such a garment, match corresponding pattern pieces at seamlines so that when the adjustment is made it will be accurate and consistent on the finished garment.

Test your adjustment in muslin, stitching it with machine basting. Make sure you have preserved the line. If your asymmetrical seam has any geometric or curved shaping, or if each angle or curve is identical your task will be further complicated. To adjust the length may mean tracing the original shapes before you adjust, then transferring them back onto the pattern after making the adjustment.

To shorten, fold out the excess along the adjustment lines or where it will least interrupt the shaping. Pin, check the adjustment, and secure with tape. Re-draw cutting lines and seamlines as indicated.

To lengthen, slash along the adjustment lines or where it will least interrupt shaping. Spread over tissue paper, pin, check adjustment, and secure with tape. Re-draw cutting lines and seamlines.

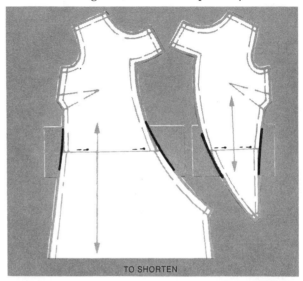

TO SHORTEN

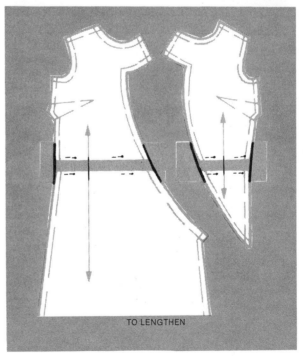

TO LENGTHEN

CURVED SEAMS: The curves that make a simple garment special can fall in the midriff, hip or lower edge area and may be distorted beyond recognition by adjusting the pattern length. *Test your adjustment in muslin*, stitching it with machine

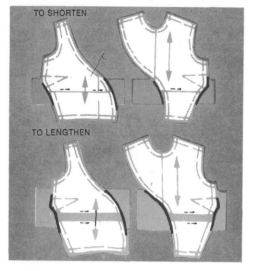

basting, to make sure you have preserved the shape. Make any further changes needed, re-stitching as often as necessary, and transfer them to your pattern pieces before cutting out your fashion fabric.

To shorten, fold out any excess along the adjustment lines, or where it will least interrupt the seamlines. Pin, check the adjustment, and secure it with tape. Re-draw the cutting lines and seamlines as indicated in the illustration.

To lengthen, slash along the adjustment lines where it will least interrupt the seamlines. Pin, check adjustment, and secure with tape. Re-draw cutting lines and seamlines as indicated.

To reduce or enlarge the circumference, all adjustments should be made on the vertical seams or the underarm area where the front joins the back. Otherwise the shapes and style lines may be noticeably distorted. If in doubt, test the changes you have made in muslin before cutting out your fashion fabric.

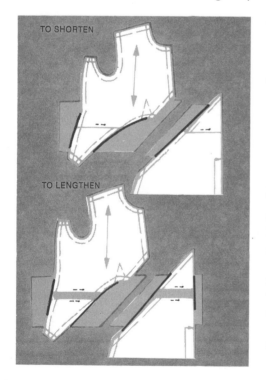

GEOMETRIC SEAMS: Angular seams that fall in the midriff, hip, or lower edge area can also be adjusted in length. *Test your adjustment in muslin*, stitching it with machine basting, to check the shape. Make any further changes needed, re-stitching as often as necessary, and transfer them to your pattern before cutting your fashion fabric.

To shorten, fold out excess length along adjustment lines, or where the least number of seamlines will be interrupted. Pin, check adjustment, and secure with tape. Re-draw cutting lines and seamlines as indicated.

To reduce or enlarge circumference, make all adjustments on vertical seams where the front joins the back. Otherwise, distortions in shape and style may occur. If in doubt, test in muslin before cutting out your fashion fabric.

Be Creative . . . Combine Two Patterns

Most women who have sewn over a period of time compile ideas that make their fashions unique expressions of themselves—they adopt a particular neckline or sleeve style that is most flattering and use it and modifications of it in many clothes they make. There must be times when you have passed up a style that you loved at first glance because a closer analysis revealed that the skirt was one that would not flatter your figure. You can overcome this problem—and achieve custom-designed clothes—by combining two or more Vogue Patterns.

The structural body relationship of shoulder to neck, bust to waist, etc. does not change within each size range of a Vogue Pattern—a size 12 bodice from one style number will fit a size 12 skirt from another style number if they both have natural waist seamlines and like silhouettes. Neckline features and sleeves too can be combined from different style numbers if the structured features of both garments are the same—for example, standard shoulder shaping with set-in sleeves, or two necklines with raglan sleeves.

The accomplished seamstress already has a comprehensive knowledge of her figure flaws and knows which styles will minimize them—she also understands the adjustments and alterations needed to adapt each pattern she uses to her needs. If you wish to stray from any of these general rules, be sure to test your experiments in muslin to avoid disappointing results after cutting into your fashion fabric.

NECKLINES: Before beginning, you should be aware of the neckline shapes most flattering to you, and whether you want to reveal or camouflage your neck and upper body. Your next consideration is bodice style, as the bodice with a sleeve variation cannot be interchanged; the shoulder and bodice of a raglan or kimono-sleeved bodice do not drape over the upper portion of the body like a bodice with set-in sleeves. Because the drape affects the neckline, you must match necklines of kimono-sleeved bodices, etc. Raised or lowered waist seamlines and other very stylized features may also affect the bodice fit and hence, the neckline.

COLLARS: There are many collars that look alike at first glance, but in reality they are not—do not be too hasty when choosing one collar style to use on another pattern design. The same pitfalls exist here as in the neckline area discussed on page 125. The necklines of two different garments may be slightly higher or lower than one another. You must make sure the bodice neck seamlines match line for line before substituting one collar for another. Also see that the closures are in the same location before making the substitution.

SLEEVES: Naturally you cannot substitute a raglan sleeve for a set-in sleeve, as the difference between the two is quite obvious. Not every set-in sleeve will fit into any bodice with that type of sleeve, as the sleeve cap length may vary greatly in style variations. The shoulder seam of the two bodices must be at the same angle and designed to end at the same point where the arm joins the body. The length of the patterns' armhole curves should also be the same.

WAIST: Determine whether the waist is raised, natural, or lowered, and whether the garment is fitted, semi-fitted, slightly fitted, or loosely fitted. These features will influence the choice of bodice and skirt combinations. The position of the waist seamlines must be the same. You can also combine styles whose bodices and skirts are cut-in-one if your garment has the same style ease at the waist. On Vogue Patterns the waist position is marked and there is a small • on each seam at the waist markings. Make sure the style lines and silhouettes are compatible and the shoulder to waist lengths are the same; some high-fitted garments, for example, have a distinctly different shape. Separate the bodices from the skirts, and join those which will create the style of your choice. Match markings carefully as you align the pattern pieces; use tape to fasten them together.

CLOSURES: There are times when you may choose a pattern with a closure that is not flattering or is unworkable for you — i.e. a back zipper in a jumpsuit or a buttoned back closure that you cannot manage without help. If this is the case, by all means use a closure that will work. Or, substitute one flattering closure for another. Most pants — and jumpsuits as well — can be zippered up the front as easily as the back. Converting a buttoned closure to a zipper closure is easy — simply make $5/8''$ seam allowances along the center markings, and then cut away the excess pattern tissue.

CONCLUSION: The fashion variety and possibilities for self-expression which result from combining patterns are endless. Always test experimental combinations in muslin to make sure you have adapted the patterns satisfactorily before translating them in a fashion fabric.

Combining Two Pattern Sizes

Those vital statistics you compiled in measuring yourself according to the directions given on pages 22–23 may reveal some interesting points—especially when compared with the "Standard Body Measurements" given on the back of each pattern envelope. You may discover that your measurements indicate that you need one pattern size for the bodice and another for the skirt; this should not surprise you, however, for there are few people whose measurements correspond exactly to those listed for a pattern size.

If you are faced with this situation, there is an easy way to expedite your adjustments—combine pattern pieces of two sizes, adjusting the waist area to your needs. Because you have chosen the two patterns to match your body measurements, the only changes needed are at the waist; this may require that you adjust one or both patterns so the waist of the garment will correspond to your needs. By using fashion patterns in this way you can create a style that is visually perfect for you and that is undistorted in the manner in which it conforms to your figure.

COMPARE MEASUREMENTS: Use the "Standard Body Measurements" on the back of the pattern envelope to note the difference between the measurements of the two sizes. This will help you arrive at the waist area changes needed when adjusting the two patterns. If your waist matches one of the sizes, half the work has been done for you, as you have only to adjust the other pattern to the correct circumference at the waist.

On the other hand, if your waist measurement indicates that both sizes need to be adjusted, determine how much each must be reduced or enlarged. Follow all the basic principles as explained on pages 100–101 for adjustments; make changes accordingly, dividing the amount needed by the number of seams.

ADJUST WAIST: When bringing the two sizes together at the waist, adjust the front and back pieces symmetrically. Keep center front and back "Place on Fold" lines and grainlines straight. Although the examples shown are basic shapes in order that style lines will not create confusion, the adjustment is easily understood and can be applied to anything you sew. Both the fitted and the A-line styles are shown in the most common situations where two sizes may be needed—a larger bodice with a smaller skirt and a smaller bodice with a larger skirt.

The adjustment is made the same as other circumference adjustments; mark ¼ the amount needed for waist at side seams of front and back pattern pieces.

For styles with a *waist seam,* adjust waist circumference of the bodice and skirt so the waist seamlines match when joined. Re-draw any darts in the skirt so their stitching lines will match those of the bodice at the waist. Be sure to retain the distance across the center of both the back and the front between darts. Re-draw darts and cutting lines as indicated or to your needs.

For *A-line* styles, cut apart both patterns along the waist markings. On Vogue Patterns the waist is identified at the centers, and a small • is placed at a corresponding spot on all remaining seams. Join the appropriate sections at the waist with tape and re-draw new cutting lines at the side seams.

WAIST SEAMED GARMENTS

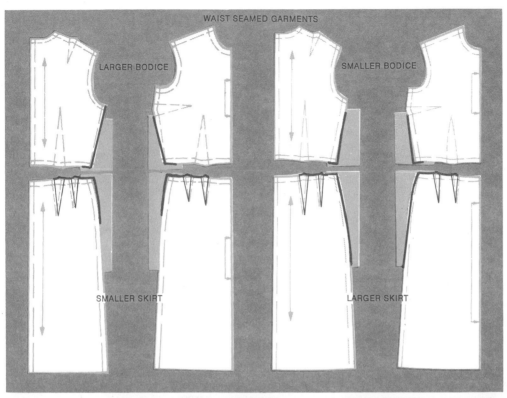

LARGER BODICE

SMALLER BODICE

SMALLER SKIRT

LARGER SKIRT

A-LINE GARMENTS

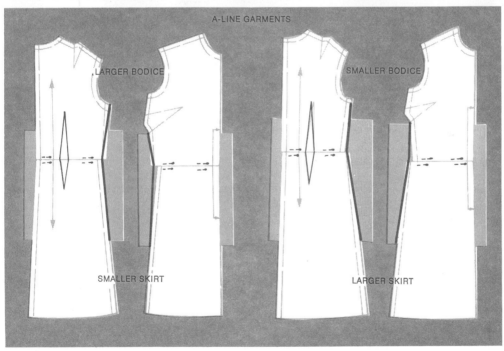

LARGER BODICE

SMALLER BODICE

SMALLER SKIRT

LARGER SKIRT

Fashion from the Ground Up: Fitting Shells

Now that you have all the facts necessary to make flat pattern adjustments, you should test the changes in muslin for accuracy. Vogue Patterns has created "Vogue's Guide to Perfect Fit of Fitted Garments"—this basic style is a fitted garment with the minimum of wearing ease built into the pattern to help you better understand your figure and analyze fit (refer to the chart on page 24). A session spent in making and fitting a muslin shell will reward you again and again with continuing perfect fit in each sewing project. It was designed to uncover figure flaws due to posture or individual body contours beyond those which, when compared with the Standard Body Measurements given for your size, necessitate adjustments in pattern length and circumference.

The construction of a basic fitting shell will provide you with a perfect sewing tool to which you can apply the knowledge gained regarding fit; it will also be an invaluable guide in making other preliminary muslins for any complex fashion garments. Use Vogue's Guide to Perfect Fit of A-line Garments if that is the style line you prefer. For pants, choose a classic cuffless, straight-legged style so you can focus on your fitting needs without distraction due to design.

The task is far from being as involved as it may seem—if your goal in fashion sewing is along haute couture lines, you will be more than well rewarded by resolving the most minute details in a muslin trial garment before cutting into your treasured fashion fabric.

A Perfect Put-on

Your muslin shell must be carefully prepared to insure accuracy of fit. The process begins with choosing a suitable fabric. Good, sturdy muslin is best—choose one that is medium weight and firm, but not crisp. However, do not feel that you are restricted to it—an old bedsheet will do just as well, providing it still has body and is not threadbare. Never use durable press fabric for your fitting shell, because if the fabric is off grain, its finish will have permanently locked the grain as it is.

PREPARATION: Pre-shrink fabric if new by washing, or press it thoroughly with a steam iron. Check the grain of your fabric—it must be straight for a garment cut from it to be fitted correctly. Straighten the ends of the fabric by pulling a crosswise thread, and cutting along it. To straighten the grain, pull fabric on the bias until the lengthwise and crosswise threads are perpendicular to one another. When satisfied that the grain is straight, mark it with a pencil on the wrong side of the fabric. Mark the lengthwise grain along the center, and the crosswise grain every half yard.

CUT OUT GARMENT: Adjust your "Vogue's Guide to Perfect Fit of Fitted Garments" pattern to your measurements; be sure to use the straight skirt rather than the A-line skirt which is also included in the pattern. Or, use a basic fashion pants pattern that has been adjusted. Arrange the fabric as indicated by your cutting layout; pin the selvages together, matching your crosswise grain markings. The fabric must be on grain before you pin the pattern pieces to it. Cut out your muslin shell carefully; even the addition of ⅛″ can distort the fit.

MARK ACCURATELY: Using a tracing wheel and dressmaker's tracing paper transfer *all* construction and position lines from your fitting pattern to your muslin. Mark seamlines, darts, bustline, and hipline. Seamlines and darts should be marked on the wrong side of the fabric; you can mark the bustline, hipline, and crosswise grain of sleeves on the right side with tracing wheel and paper, or you can mark them on the wrong side and transfer them to the right side with thread tracing after the pattern pieces have been removed. Make sure your thread tracing is clearly visible; choose one color for position lines and other colors for the lengthwise grain, center folds, and crosswise grain. You should be able to identify each of these, as well as position lines, at a glance on the bodice, skirt, and sleeves, as well as on each pants leg.

CONSTRUCT GARMENT: Follow the sewing instructions of your pattern when making your muslin fitting garment. For fashion garments, eliminate all facings, pockets, etc. and use only the bodice, skirt, and sleeve pattern pieces for dresses; for pants, use the front and back pattern pieces only.

Stitch the garment sections together with machine basting so changes can be made with relative ease in minimal time. Stitch the neck and lower edges of sleeves along the seamlines. Turn in the edges along the stitching; clip as necessary, then baste and press. The zipper is machine basted in place so you will be able to easily try on and fit your muslin shell.

The waist edge of pants should be staystitched to prevent its stretching. Baste the zipper in place so you can easily try on and fit your pants. To support the pants during fitting, cut 1″ wide grosgrain ribbon the length of your adjusted waistband, and transfer the markings to it. Then baste it to the pants, placing one edge along the waist seamline.

A Brief Try-on

Now is the time to try on your muslin fitting shell or your pants fitting muslin and begin to finalize a perfect fit. With your muslin on, stand in front of a full-length mirror. With a critical eye, review the relationship of the fit of your garment to your body. The following check list consists of points to evaluate in determining the necessity of further alterations in your **basic muslin fitting shell** in order to achieve a perfect fit. Analyze them carefully and with objectivity.

☐ The muslin garment should be balanced on the body. Lengthwise grainlines, side seams, and center front and center back seams or markings should hang straight and be perpendicular to the floor.

☐ Test for the comfort of wearing ease while sitting, moving, and bending. Raise and lower arms to further test mobility.

☐ The garment length from neck to waist and from waist to hem should be in proportion to your figure.

☐ Crosswise grainlines and the waist seams should be parallel to the floor, and at right angles to center seams or markings.

☐ The neckline should smoothly encircle the base of the neck and should have enough ease for normal, comfortable movement. It should neither bind nor be loose.

☐ Shoulder seams must be straight and directly on top of the shoulder. They should mold the shoulder smoothly, and extend from the base of the neck to the tip of the shoulder bone without wavering or distortion.

☐ Darts should be properly positioned and should point toward the apex of each bust curve.

☐ The armhole should curve smoothly over the end of the shoulder bone and the underarm seamline at its lowest point should be 1″ below the armpit.

☐ The entire garment should mold smoothly over the body without wrinkling, pulling, or straining at any point. It should fit smoothly and attractively, and should provide enough wearing ease for you to move comfortably and without restriction or binding.

☐ The lengthwise grain of sleeves from shoulder to elbow should be perpendicular to the floor. The sleeve must be smooth and wrinkle-free.

☐ The hem should be even—any distortion indicates the need for alterations.

PANTS: Apply what you have learned regarding the analysis of the fit of your basic muslin fitting shell. Here are the additional elements to which you should be attuned when analyzing the effects on fit of the adjustments you have made:

☐ Side and inseams should hang straight and be perpendicular to the floor. The grain should be undistorted.

☐ All horizontal position markings should be parallel to the floor.

☐ Each pants leg should hang smoothly and should not restrict any part of your leg. There should be no strained or baggy areas.

☐ The crotch seam should follow your body contour and be smooth and balanced over its entire length.

☐ The crotch should be the correct depth—neither too low and baggy, nor too high and binding.

☐ Evaluate the proposed hem length of your pants while wearing shoes of the proper heel height—any change here could cause the front of your pants to break above the instep or the back of pants to drag.

CONCLUSION: In making your flat pattern adjustments, you have brought your fitting shell into proportion with your figure. Because they are based upon measurements alone, these adjustments cannot be expected to accommodate the body curves and planes which are unique to you. If your adjusted fitting shell has not passed the visual and physical tests of fit under your careful scrutiny, you must delve into Book III to resolve those fitting problems which are related to your individual contours. It will be through these further personal alterations that you can expect to achieve a basic muslin fitting shell in which perfect fit is a reality and which will be your most fundamental sewing tool.

Surrounding Yourself With Fashion Fit

Alterations
Structuring Fit
In Personal Terms

You may ask yourself why alterations should be considered when you adjusted your pattern to your measurements before cutting it out. Our reply consists of a question—why be satisfied with only mediocre or satisfactory fit when you can have perfect fit that corresponds exactly to your contours? The key words that distinguish adjustments and alterations are **measurements** and **contours.** The closest you can come to perfect fit by adjusting your pattern pieces without making alterations too is what your tape measure can tell you about your measurements in relation to those of your pattern. You can accurately adjust your pattern pieces to your length and circumference measurements and achieve a reasonably good fit. However, a tape measure and a flat pattern piece alone come nowhere near incorporating the contours of your body.

Vogue Patterns appreciates and shares your concern with attaining perfect fit and goes to great lengths to offer the easiest possible methods for altering and personalizing the fit of your pattern. After your muslin fitting shell has been altered, transfer these personal fitting changes to your pattern pieces; this completes the process of total pattern adaptation and eliminates the need for making a muslin fitting shell for every succeeding garment you make.

Because the bust area is the most difficult to fit and because your bust measurement is a good indication of your other body proportions, we recommend purchasing your patterns according to bust circumference. Although you may have heard it suggested that you choose your pattern size in relation to your frame only, this would invariably require major alterations in order to accommodate your particular body contours.

We suggest that your frame be a point of consideration—but not the sole basis—when you select the pattern size of your muslin fitting shell; if you fall between sizes, choose the next larger size if your frame is large or the next smaller size if your frame is small. In selecting a size close to your **circumference** measurements, your pattern will essentially fit you from the beginning, and thus eliminate the drastic pattern adjustments and major alterations required when you choose a pattern size on the basis of **frame** alone. Adjusting the flat pattern to your measurements will bring you closer to perfect fit. Constructing a muslin fitting shell from your adjusted pattern and then altering it to conform perfectly to your contours ensures the ultimate in haute couture fit for your fashions.

Limit your alterations to the minimum by starting with a muslin fitting shell which has been adjusted to your length and circumference measurements; this will enable you to easily transfer your alterations to any garment design. Minor alterations can be transferred to other styles while retaining the original design lines of the garment. The major alterations which would be required in altering a fitting shell whose size was related only to your frame can also be transferred to other styles. However, such extreme changes in fit can often irreparably destroy the original lines of the design you intend to make, especially if this is to any extent complicated or involves many pattern pieces.

Remember too, that two other factors will help to eliminate the need for alterations: good posture and maintaining a weight appropriate for your frame. We have stressed these points in the fitting section of this book and they are excellent ones to keep in mind.

Getting Into Alterations

If you are fortunate enough to have a figure that corresponds to those on which the pattern industry bases its standard sizes, you may find only slight alterations are needed to achieve perfect fit. You may, in this case, correct minor fitting problems in your muslin as you would in the fashion fabric following the instructions in Book I. Transfer the changes to your fitting pattern. Do not attempt this, however, unless the alterations needed are *minimal* and can be achieved easily in darts and seam allowances. For the majority of the sewing population, the following alterations in Book III will correct any figure flaws you may have.

We have arranged alteration procedures in a logical sequence to make perfect fit a reality for you by understanding the reasoning and the principles behind fitting any garment. To simplify instructions, there are before and after illustrations of fitting problems which illustrate first, the evidence of poor fit in a particular area, and second, the problem area after it has been corrected. Each section on altering a specific area includes the pattern piece, the correct adjustment as it would appear transferred to your pattern and *bold lines* to indicate interrupted cutting or dart lines. Be sure to read pages 100–101 if you need help in interpreting the pattern changes. Circumference alterations are much like circumference adjustments. Alterations for dresses are handled in this chapter; pants are covered in a separate section.

Other popular styles—like raglan and kimono sleeve designs—are illustrated in adjusted pattern pieces whenever an alteration applies to these garments.

The most important point to keep in mind when altering your garment is accuracy. You must be both patient and thorough in order to be accurate. Fitting procedures done hurriedly or haphazardly can never attain the same quality of well planned and patiently executed alterations. Take your time, accept the challenge of alterations in the proper spirit, and work toward achieving perfect fit. When your changes have been completed, we will tell you how to make your master pattern a permanent sewing tool to use for every garment you sew (see pages 182–185).

Shoulders

Begin with the shoulders in shaping your muslin fitting shell to the contours of your body and keeping the direction of the grainlines correct. In styles with the sleeve and shoulder combined—like raglan and kimono sleeves—grain is an equally important consideration. When the grain is correct in the shoulder area, it is a good indication that your fitting shell will hang straight from the shoulders. There may be other body areas which distort the direction of the grain, but these figure flaws are easily remedied if the proper grain has been established in the shoulder area. The shoulder seams should be directly on top of the shoulders and end at the arm hinge and at the base of the neck.

SQUARE SHOULDERS: Caused by bone structure, this variation is evidenced by pulling around the shoulder and armhole area because the garment is not wide enough to accommodate your body. Remove the sleeve and slash both front and back bodice sections near the shoulder seam from armhole edge to neck seamline. By adding the necessary amount of fabric equally—half the amount needed in the back, and half in the front—you retain the proper positioning of the shoulder seam and the original direction of the grain. Spread cut edges the amount needed for proper fit—smooth any wrinkles as you mold the muslin. Insert strips of fabric under the cut edges and baste. Trim strips even with armhole edge. Raise armhole the amount added to shoulder area and re-shape. Transfer alterations to pattern.

To alter a yoke, slash along shoulder marking to neck seamline Alter raglan sleeves and princess styles as indicated. For a kimono sleeve, slash across the pattern so you can raise the shoulder curves; correct armhole curve. Test these styles in muslin *before* cutting out your fashion fabric.

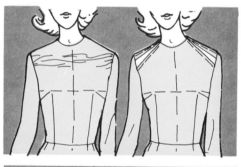

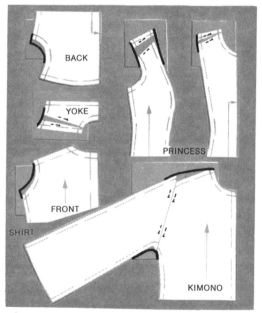

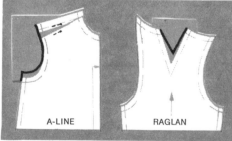

SLOPING SHOULDERS: Due to bone structure, sloping shoulders may be more apparent when combined with poor posture, but they are essentially caused by the angle of the shoulder bone in relation to the neck and the arm. The muslin wrinkles near the bust dart and across the end of the shoulder in the back. These wrinkles are easily eliminated by molding the fabric to the correct angle of your shoulder and shaping the armhole to the set of your arm.

There are two methods of correcting this problem. First, try shoulder pads of varying shapes, widths, and thicknesses when you are planning to alter sloping shoulders in jackets, coats, and other outerwear styles. The use of shoulder pads in a coat dress or shirt-style jacket in a medium weight fabric may also be the answer to the problem. However, a dress, blouse, or vest in a light- to medium weight fabric will not benefit from the use of shoulder pads—in most knit fabrics they would be disastrous.

If shoulder pads do not correct the problem, you must alter the muslin to fit your shoulders. For set-in sleeves, remove the sleeve. Pin out excess at the shoulder, tapering to the neck seamline. Lower the armhole seamline the same amount as the excess fabric removed from the shoulder. This re-shaping retains the original size of the armhole and does not change the fit of the set-in sleeve. Transfer the alteration to your pattern.

To alter a garment design with a yoke, slash along shoulder markings from the armhole edge to neck seamline to reduce the amount needed. Re-shape the armhole as you did for a set-in sleeve. For raglan sleeves and princess-style garments, alter pattern piece as indicated in the illustration below. However, for the kimono sleeve, first slash across pattern so that you can reduce the shoulder curve more easily, and then correct the armhole curve to fit properly. Always test these styles in muslin *before* you begin cutting out your fashion fabric.

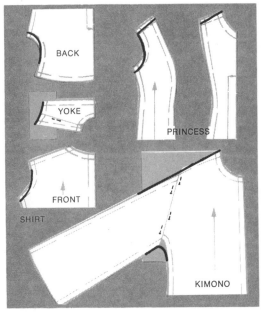

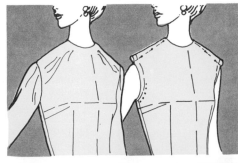

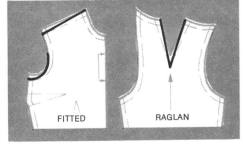

NARROW SHOULDERS: This alteration is necessitated by bone structure, too, and the fitting shell must be taken in at the front shoulder area as well as the back. In set-in sleeves, the armhole seams fall beyond the shoulder point; other sleeve styles wrinkle across the upper arm and sometimes restrict movement. Correct set-in sleeve designs by pinning a dart in the front and back, pulling armhole seam to correct position. Alter pattern pieces the same amount.

To alter a yoke with a set-in sleeve, slash midway through the yoke at shoulder markings and through yoke and into front and back sections; you must decrease the shoulder length. Make a fold, tapering to nothing at armhole seamline. Alter other sleeve types and style variations as shown. Test in muslin *before* cutting into your fashion fabric.

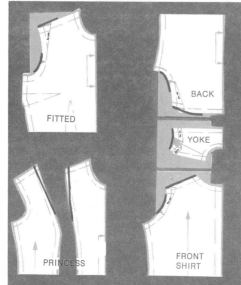

FITTED

BACK

YOKE

PRINCESS

FRONT
SHIRT

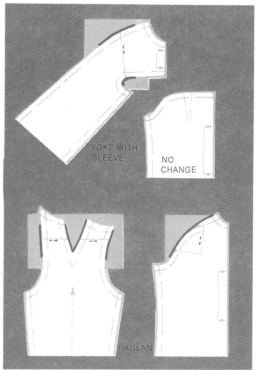

YOKE WITH
SLEEVE

NO
CHANGE

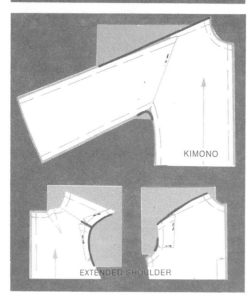

KIMONO

EXTENDED SHOULDER

RAGLAN

BROAD SHOULDERS: The alteration is needed to accommodate bone structure. Set-in sleeve styles are pulled at the sleeve cap as the armhole seams are drawn up over broad shoulders. Other sleeve styles are pulled in the armhole area and movement is restricted. Correct your fitting shell by slashing front and back sections from a point midway along the shoulder to armhole seam. Spread cut edges until shoulder area is smooth and properly molded. Insert fabric strips under cut edges and baste.

For a yoke alteration with set-in sleeves, slash midway through the yoke at shoulder markings and again from the shoulder to the armhole seamline of front and back sections. Spread as needed. Alter pattern pieces as shown below for other sleeve types and style variations. Test in muslin *before* cutting into your fashion fabric.

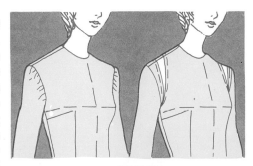

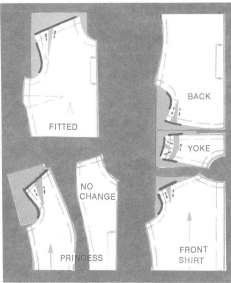

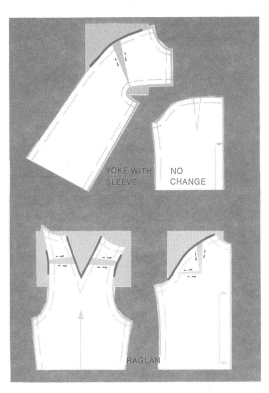

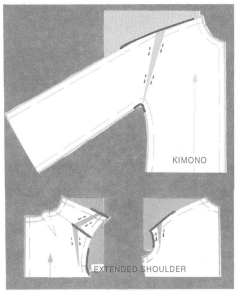

Necklines

A neckline is often a primary focal point of your garment. What the rest of your garment does for your body, the neckline does for your face. To flatter you, it must not only be an appropriate style but also a superb fit.

The base of your neck is the point from which any garment neckline is designed, and is either raised or lowered. Your muslin "Vogue's Guide to Perfect Fit Pattern" has a "jewel" neckline, which follows the base of the neck. It provides the fundamental neckline fit; your fashion pattern necklines can be adapted to the alterations explained here. A neckline that constricts or hangs away from you is not attractive or flattering to your face or fashion.

TIGHT NECKLINE: The neckline pulls and cuts into the neck. The top edge of your garment reaches far above the base of the neck, binding and stretching your fabric. To bring the neckline into position, draw a line on the fabric where the neckline of the muslin shell should be, and stitch along this line. Clip to this line every ½″

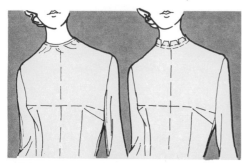

until it is comfortable. Transfer your alteration to your pattern (alter facings as well) by drawing in new cutting lines the distance of the new seamline from the original. Make the same alterations in set-in sleeve garments with yokes, and in raglan and kimono sleeves that have jewel necklines. Test these styles in muslin *before* you cut out your fashion fabric.

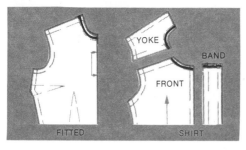

LARGE NECKLINE: The neckline hangs loosely and does not reach the base of the neck. To raise the neckline, baste a folded shaped bias strip of fabric in the

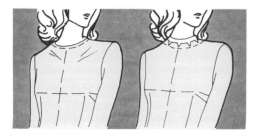

correct position. Alter bodice front as indicated on page 143, making the same change on bodice back and facings. You can apply the same alteration to a yoke garment with a set-in sleeve, and to raglan and kimono sleeves with a jewel neckline. Always test these styles in muslin *before* you cut into your fashion fabric.

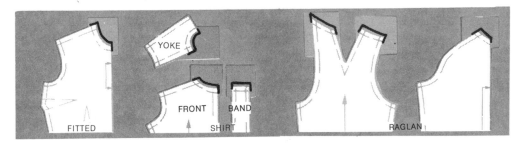

GAPING NECKLINE: Wrong bust cup size, hollow chest, pigeon chest, or a pattern that is too small can create a neckline that gapes. Cut bodice in muslin to locate the problem—both gaping and pulling can be present concurrently. Even though your pattern is purchased by bust measurement, your bust cup size or body contours may still distort necklines. Often a combination of alterations is necessary to fit the neckline properly; the problem here would be evident in square, V- or U-necklines; they should be tested in the same manner.

Excess Fabric: Too much fabric causes the neckline to stand away from the body in wrinkles above the bust. Smooth out the wrinkles and pin, tapering to the armhole seam. To make the changes on your pattern, lower cutting line at the shoulder half the amount needed, tapering to the armhole seam. Raise the center front the other half of amount needed. Make same change on facing. Alter similarly for raglan sleeves and kimono sleeves.

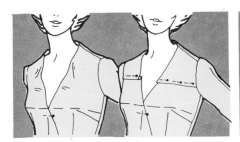
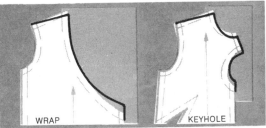

Pulling: In this type of gaping neckline, the armhole seam pulls and distorts the neckline above the bust. To alter, release the armhole seam in that area and slash the muslin from where it pulls at the armhole to the neck seamline. Spread the muslin as needed, and baste in strips of fabric. Re-baste sleeve to test. Alter your pattern by slashing in the same manner. Make the same change on facing. Alter raglan and kimono sleeves similarly.

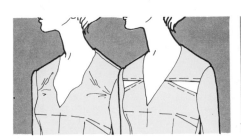
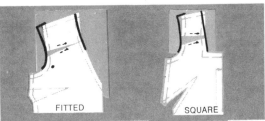

143

Skimpy: Too little fabric to cover the bust contour will cause the neckline to pull and gape. The bodice front must be altered to bring the neckline into correct position. Refer to the alteration for the large bust cup on pages 156–157. Maintain your bodice design in correcting the fit.

DÉCOLLETÉ OR LOW NECKLINES: To bring your neckline to the position you want *before* you cut into your fashion fabric; cut and make a muslin neck facing. Then stitch along the seamline. Turn in neck edges along the stitching and clip every ½"; baste. Try on the facing, checking to see how deep the neckline is. To raise the neckline, fill it in with a piece of fabric until the desired depth is achieved. Re-draw cutting lines on facing and bodice front, maintaining the style lines.

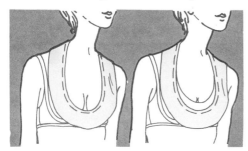
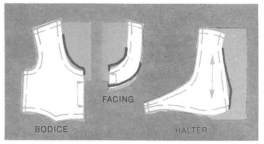

Sleeveless Armholes

Although your basic fitting shell has a set-in sleeve, there are many sleeveless styles—close-fitting armholes, cut-away armholes, or halter variations. To ensure a perfect fit in these styles, we suggest constructing a muslin bodice from your pattern. Alterations required in the armhole area may be the result of poor fit in other areas. Proper fit in the shoulder area, as well as in the back, chest, and bust areas should be achieved *before* altering the armhole area (refer to the appropriate alteration sections for these).

Cut-away armholes and the armhole area of a halter neckline are not as close to the arm, and the shape is not the same as a close-fitting sleeveless armhole. There is little or no wearing ease in the shoulder and side underarm seams as the fit of these armholes depends largely upon the support of the body.

Test the fit of an armhole by stitching along the armhole seamline. Turn seam allowance to the inside along the stitching and clip at ½" to ¾" intervals; baste. Try on the bodice and check the underarm portion—the classic sleeveless armhole should fit close to the body and should be 1" below the armpit. The rest of the armhole should fit smoothly without pulling, binding, or restricting movement.

TIGHT ARMHOLE: If the armhole is too tight it will bind and pull from the underarm to below the shoulder. Re-draw the armhole seamline further into the body of the garment on front and back sections where the binding occurs. Remove bodice and basting stitches. Stitch carefully along new seamline and clip at ½" intervals; baste. Try on bodice once more to see that no further alterations are necessary, and that the new armhole is smooth and comfortable. Transfer the alteration to bodice and facing pattern pieces as indicated on the illustration for bodice.

Alter the pattern of a cut-away armhole and the armhole area of a halter as indicated. Test the alteration in muslin **before** cutting into your fashion fabric in order to resolve this problem with confidence.

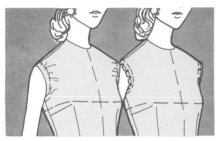

FITTED   HALTER   CUT-AWAY

LARGE ARMHOLE: In sleeveless styles this alteration is required primarily in the underarm area when the armhole is too deep. To correct, insert bias strips of fabric to fill in the amount needed around and under the arm. When these strips are placed accurately, they should produce an even extension of the underarm seam, as well as retain the proper curve of the armhole. Baste strips securely in place. Transfer the alteration to bodice and facing pattern pieces.

Alter the pattern of a cut-away armhole and the armhole area of a halter as indicated. Test in muslin **before** cutting into your fashion fabric.

FITTED   HALTER   CUT-AWAY

GAPING ARMHOLES: Even though your muslin bodice fits smoothly in the shoulders before altering the armhole, further alteration of this area may be required if the armhole gapes. For a closer armhole fit, pin out excess fabric at the shoulder to bring the armhole into place. Taper shoulder seam to the neck. If this alteration does not correct the armhole, you may have to further raise the underarm by inserting bias strips, as you would in altering a large armhole.

Alter the pattern of a cut-away armhole and the armhole area of a halter as indicated. Test in muslin **before** cutting into your fashion fabric.

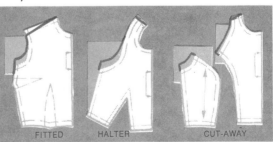

FITTED   HALTER   CUT-AWAY

Sleeves

Since sleeves are an integral part of your garment, they should fit well and be visually pleasing. Countless variations of sleeves can be found in the Vogue Patterns catalog. Sleeves are grouped into three types: ***set-in,*** joined with a seam that encircles the arm near the shoulder; ***raglan,*** with diagonal seaming that extends to the neck edge; and ***kimono,*** cut-in-one with the garment.

Set-in sleeve versions are innumerable: the classic one- or two-piece sleeve in any length you may choose, as well as the shirt, bishop, angel, bell and trumpet styles which usually have a smooth sleeve cap. These can also be gathered in the sleeve cap area and anywhere along the arm to create a puff sleeve or can be combined with a fitted sleeve to create a leg-of-mutton sleeve.

Raglan sleeves can be one- or two-piece, and are great problem-solvers for hard-to-fit shoulders. Not only can a good fit be achieved with these sleeves, but they involve less handling during construction than the other types.

Kimono sleeves exist in nearly as many variations as the set-in: they can be used with gussets for a high-fitting armhole, or can be cut without a shoulder and upper arm seam for loose, flowing styles. There is the cap sleeve version, a yoke cut-in-one with any length of sleeve, the dolman, the bat-wing, etc.

With a better understanding of sleeves, you will certainly approach them with greater awareness. Once you have worked out your problems in three basic types it will be a simple matter to alter any of the variations. It should not surprise you that there are as many different types of arms as there are deviations from standard body measurements.

Often body fit on a pattern is refined to satisfaction, yet the sleeves are neglected because fitting them is considered difficult and troublesome. This is unfortunate, as sleeve fit is an integral part of perfect fit and is not complicated at all. Frequently, sleeve fit is distorted by nothing more than the ease distribution of the sleeve cap being inappropriate for your body contour or bone structure. The sleeves of Vogue patterns are designed for a standard figure; you must individualize your pattern by building in your own sleeve fit.

EASE DISTRIBUTION: Simple to correct, this problem is visible when the upper sleeve area will not lie smoothly and diagonal wrinkles will form at the front or back of the sleeve cap and continue across the sleeve, distorting the lengthwise grain. To alter, release the sleeve between the notches. For wrinkles that start at the front of

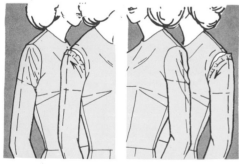

the sleeve cap, re-adjust the ease, shifting it toward the front until the wrinkles are eliminated. For wrinkles that start at the back of the sleeve cap, shift the ease toward the back, re-distributing it until the wrinkles have been eliminated. To check the alteration you have made, baste the sleeve into the armhole and re-examine it with care. The upper sleeve area should now be smooth.

SKIMPY SLEEVE CAP: The sleeve cap is too short, causing it to pull and collapse, creating wrinkles. Remove sleeve between notches, slash across the sleeve. Place a piece of fabric under the cut edges, spreading the amount needed to increase cap. Re-baste to check. Alter the pattern as indicated.

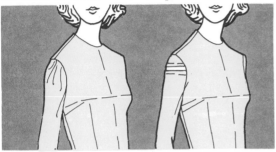 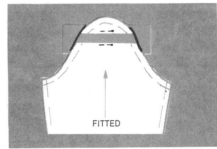

SLEEVE CAP TOO DEEP: Wrinkles appear across the top of the sleeve cap just under the seam. To correct, pin out the excess fabric until it lies flat. On the pattern, fold out the same amount on the sleeve cap. You should expect to have less ease in the cap as a result of this correction.

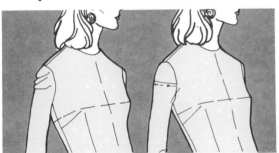 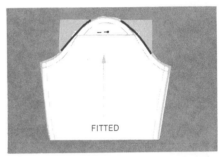

EXCESS EASE: Wrinkles appear in the sleeve cap around the armhole seam, distorting the sleeve shape. Rip out the stitching between notches at sleeve cap. Smooth out the wrinkles and pin in a shallow vertical dart. Baste sleeve in place. To correct pattern, slash at the shoulder marking 3″–4″ down, and lap edges the amount to be decreased. The pattern will bulge slightly; to make the seam allowances lie flat, clip 1½″ at each end of eased area. Check to make sure the circumference of the sleeve is preserved under the eased area. Shorten the sleeve cap slightly by drawing a new cutting line.

 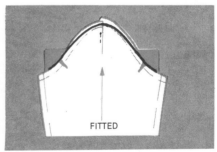

LARGE ARM: A fitted sleeve that is not altered to fit a large arm will have absolutely no wearing ease and be uncomfortable. The sleeve will pull and bind due to lack of sufficient fabric in the sleeve. Even though the armhole is adequate, there still is not enough room for a well-developed or fleshy arm. To enlarge the sleeve, slash along the lengthwise grain. Spread the slash over a strip of fabric as needed, allowing for wearing ease and tapering to the shoulder seam and to the sleeve edge. If, when enlarging the circumference, the sleeve cap is still distorted, alter the sleeve cap the same as you would for skimpy sleeve cap, page 147. Test alterations. When altering the pattern, form tucks as shown to make the pattern lie flat. Re-draw sleeve cap and grainlines.

Stylized versions of the set-in sleeve such as the bell or shirt will need this alteration too. Alter a raglan sleeve in the same way. A gathered shirt sleeve with a cuff can be altered in both girth and length to create a longer, fuller sleeve that is more in proportion with your figure. To enlarge a kimono sleeve, add half the amount needed to both front and back seam edges as indicated. Be sure to test these alterations in muslin *before* cutting out your fashion fabric.

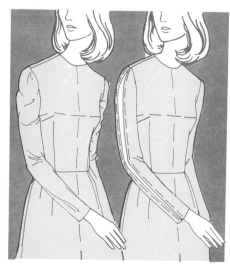

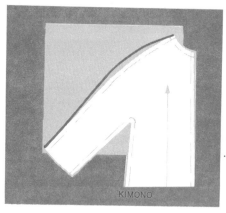

KIMONO

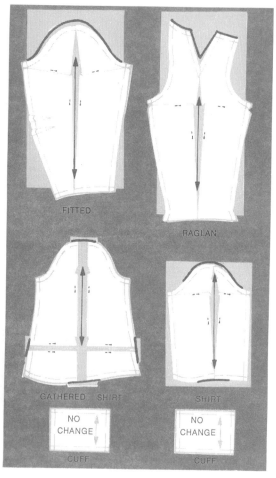

FITTED

RAGLAN

GATHERED SHIRT

SHIRT

NO CHANGE

NO CHANGE

CUFF

CUFF

148

THIN ARM: A fitted sleeve on a thin arm will wrinkle and sag. Wearing ease becomes bagginess and the sleeve has no fitted shape. While the too-large sleeve may feel comfortable, its appearance will ruin your fashion impact. To correct, make a lengthwise fold along the lengthwise grain, starting at the sleeve cap and tapering to the lower edge. Be sure there is enough width to allow the hand to slip through the sleeves if no opening is provided. To transfer the alteration to the pattern, make an identical change. Sleeve ease will be somewhat lessened by the fold.

Style variations of the set-in sleeve, such as shirt or bishop, will need this alteration too. A gathered shirt sleeve can be altered in both girth and length to create a narrower and shorter sleeve that is more in proportion with your figure. To reduce a raglan sleeve, make a fold from the dart to the sleeve edge. On a kimono sleeve, reduce both seam edges as shown, halving the amount needed and making an equal adjustment on both the front and back. Be sure to test these alterations in muslin *before* cutting out your fashion fabric.

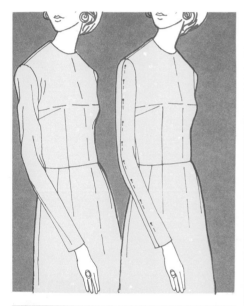

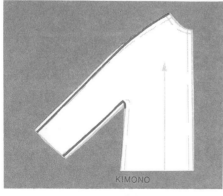

KIMONO

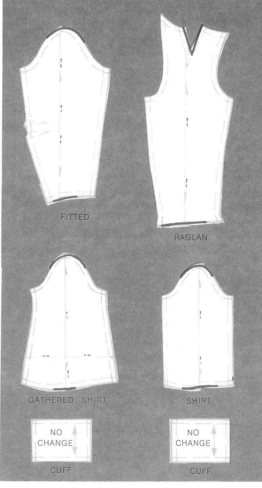

FITTED

RAGLAN

GATHERED SHIRT

SHIRT

NO CHANGE

CUFF

NO CHANGE

CUFF

149

LARGE UPPER ARM: A sleeve inadequate for a large upper arm will be snug above the elbow and the armhole seam will bind. Wearing ease will be non-existent, and the look will be distorted. To correct, release the stitching between the notches on the sleeve cap. Slash along the grainline and insert a strip of fabric under the slash. Spread the sleeve the amount needed—allow wearing ease as well—and baste. Extend the ease on the sleeve cap beyond the markings 1″–2″ so it will be well distributed; re-baste the sleeve into the armhole. Try on the muslin shell to check the fit. If you find the armhole seam still binds, refer to page 138 and make the alteration for square shoulders. Transfer the alteration to the fitting pattern, re-drawing the grainline as indicated.

Make the same alteration for a short sleeve or a slim shirt sleeve with a cuff, and a raglan sleeve. Slash kimono sleeve at shoulder indication and down as shown to alter, adding half the amount needed to the front and half to the back. Test these in muslin *before* cutting into your fashion fabric.

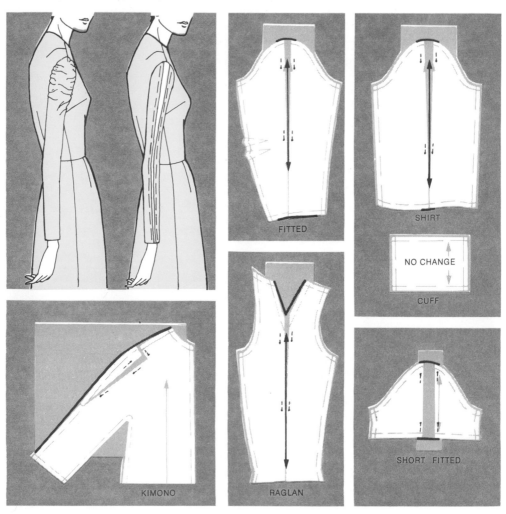

FITTED

SHIRT

NO CHANGE

CUFF

KIMONO

RAGLAN

SHORT FITTED

THICK ELBOW: Although ease, shape, or darts in fitted sleeves allow elbow movement, often the sleeve just cannot accommodate a large, thick elbow. The sleeve pulls from the shoulder and is uncomfortable. At the elbow itself, the fit is tight and binding. To correct, release stitching between the notches on the sleeve seam. Starting between the darts, slash to the grainline, then continue upward along the grainline to the sleeve cap edge. Place strips of fabric under the slashed edges and spread the amount needed; baste. To take up extra fabric at the sleeve seam, add a dart between any existing ones. Re-stitch sleeve seam and try on to check fit. Transfer the alteration to the pattern, and draw in the added dart.

To alter stylized set-in sleeves such as a slim shirt sleeve with a cuff, slash as indicated. Alter a raglan or kimono sleeve pattern in the same manner, slashing through the center of the elbow ease if darts are not used. Because these designs may involve an unusual distribution of style ease, it is always wise to test your alteration in muslin *before* cutting out your fashion fabric.

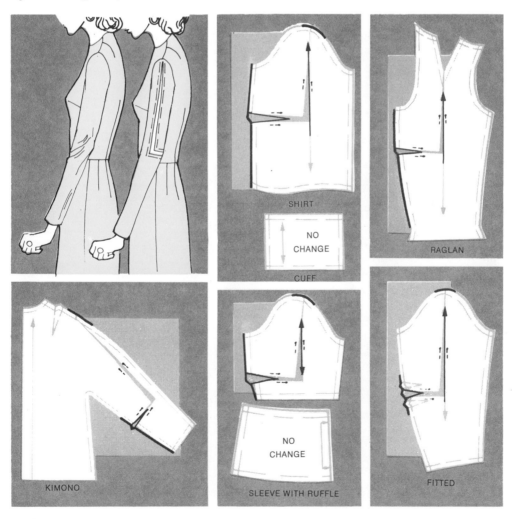

SHIRT

NO CHANGE

CUFF

RAGLAN

KIMONO

NO CHANGE

SLEEVE WITH RUFFLE

FITTED

LARGE FOREARM: A large forearm will cause the sleeve to pull and bind below the elbow; movement will be restricted on a garment with a fitted sleeve. The fullness of the arm will also use up wearing ease and will emphasize the large forearm. To alter your muslin, slash along the grainline from the lower edge up toward the sleeve cap. Place a fabric strip under the slash and spread the amount needed, adding some wearing ease for insured comfort. Baste the strip in place and try on to check fit. Transfer the alteration to the pattern.

For a shorter, close-fitting sleeve with fashion detail at the edge, the trim must be adjusted too. For a raglan sleeve, slash along the grainline from the lower edge up to the dart. For a kimono sleeve, add ¼ the amount needed at each sleeve edge. Test in muslin **before** cutting into your fashion fabric.

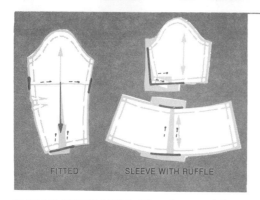

FITTED   SLEEVE WITH RUFFLE

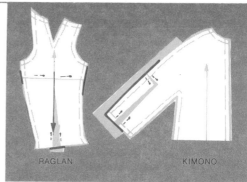

RAGLAN   KIMONO

SMALL FOREARM: If a sleeve without stylized trim—like a cuff or band that hugs the wrist—is too large due to a small forearm, it hangs loosely and drapes in wrinkles below the elbow. The sleeve design is distorted and can ruin the lines of the entire garment. To take in the lower sleeve, fold out the excess, tapering the fold up from the lower edge. Always be sure that you have allowed enough room in the sleeve for your hand to slip through. Do not fold out wearing ease. Transfer the alteration to the pattern as indicated.

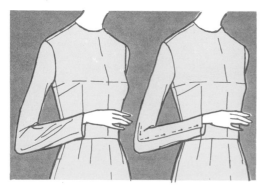

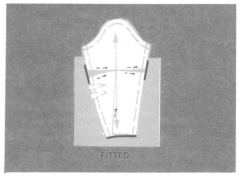

FITTED

Alter a raglan sleeve the same as you would the fitted sleeve on page 152.

For a kimono sleeve, mark ¼ the amount to be decreased at both seam edges; draw in new cutting lines, tapering to armhole. Test these alterations in muslin **before** cutting into your fashion fabric.

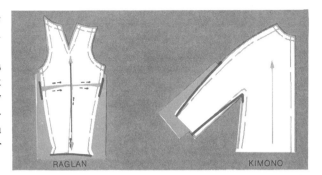

RAGLAN   KIMONO

Bust

The bust is one of the most important body areas to be fitted correctly. For this reason, Vogue Patterns suggests that you buy all your patterns—dresses, blouses, jackets, coats, etc.—by bust measurement to provide the correct circumference for this crucial body area. Other flat pattern adjustments and alterations can then be made with relative ease.

Even though adequate circumference has been supplied, the bust area may need alterations for other reasons. The position of the bust may be either high or low; the bust cup may be larger or smaller than that of the standard figure; or your proportions may have demanded concessions in pattern size. **Before** you examine the bust area, check the fit of your shoulders, neckline, sleeves, and armholes. This is the best way to proceed toward your goal of perfect fit, as it takes into consideration the combination of your basic frame and your actual proportions, and the effect that both of these will have on clothing.

Fitting techniques which are based initially on the fit of any area other than the bust make fitting more difficult than it has to be. In accommodating the bust with the least amount of fitting, style lines will never be distorted as they would if you bought your pattern to fit your frame, and then attempted to fit this pattern to your actual curves.

A woman's bustline can enhance or detract from her appearance, depending on the fit she builds into her garments. When you try on your muslin shell, determine whether or not you need any bustline alterations. Often, the contours and bone structure of your **back** can subtract the necessary circumference from the bust, making the fit tight and uncomfortable. Check to see if this is your particular bust fit problem before making any alterations. Turn to page 163 for alterations to fit the back. When fitting the bust, there are several points you must look for in order to make the correct alterations:

☐ Examine the shoulders, neckline, and sleeves of your garment for proper fit before beginning to make any needed alterations in the bust area.

☐ The fitting difficulty should be with the bustline, rather than the **back**.

☐ Where do the points of the bust darts lie? The underarm dart should end ½″ from the apex and the front darts ½″–1″ below the apex.

☐ Wear the proper undergarments when determining whether to alter.

☐ Never over-fit. A too-tight bust fit will be very uncomfortable.

BUST WITH SMALL CUP: Although a pattern may be purchased by bust size, a bust area with a small cup may need to be altered to fit smoothly. Excess fabric causes wrinkles over the bust apex, giving an unkempt appearance. To reduce the bust area on your fitting muslin, pin out the excess fabric, making folds parallel and at right angles to the grainline. Be sure to retain wearing ease in both the front and the back. Taper horizontal folds to the side seams and vertical folds to the waist; taper lower for A-line garments. Transfer alteration to pattern. On A-line styles, slash through the center of the dart to allow the edges to overlap. If the tapering extends below waist, add to the seams the amount taken out in the skirt section to preserve hip circumference.

In all darted styles, the darts will become shorter and narrower; fit them to your bust proportions (see pages 159–160), re-drawing as needed.

For styles whose bust shaping is created by seaming details rather than darts, place your altered fitting pattern underneath the pattern as a guide. Reduce the bust by making horizontal and vertical folds, as shown; draw in all broken cutting lines. Be sure to test in muslin *before* cutting into your fashion fabric.

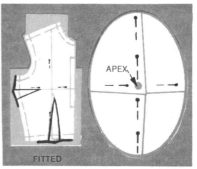

FITTED

APEX

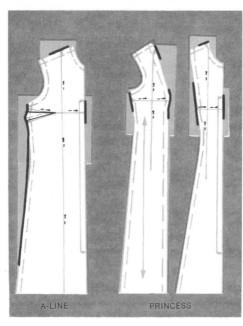

A-LINE   PRINCESS

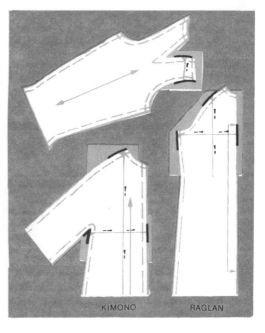

KIMONO   RAGLAN

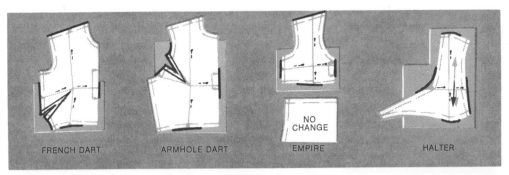

FRENCH DART ARMHOLE DART EMPIRE HALTER

NO CHANGE

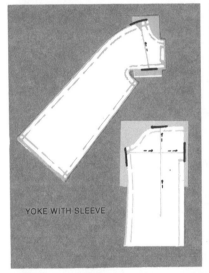

YOKE WITH SLEEVE

YOKED

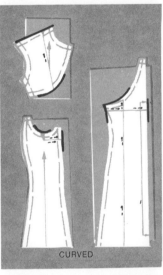

CURVED

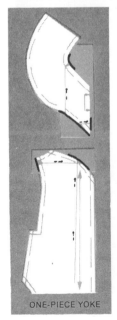

ONE-PIECE YOKE

FRONT INSET

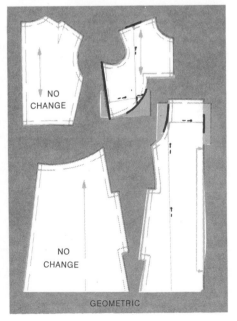

NO CHANGE

NO CHANGE

GEOMETRIC

BUST WITH LARGE CUP: Many women with a large bust cup find that it is necessary to enlarge the bust area of their garments to accommodate the extra fullness. The bodice pulls and is tight across the bust, flattening the apex. To alter your muslin to fit your contours, slash through the bust darts and across the front, as shown, at a right angle to the grainline. Slash parallel to the grainline down the front from the shoulder through the apex to the waist seam (or lower, for an A-line fitting muslin). Spread the bodice muslin the amount that is needed. Be careful not to over-fit. Insert and baste strips of fabric in place. Make the alteration on the pattern in the same manner. Re-draw darts, deepening them and changing their length to correspond to your figure (see pages 159–160). After being stitched, trim the darts 5/8″ from the lines of stitching to reduce the bulk, if necessary. Press the darts open.

To make this alteration in garments whose bust shaping is created by seaming details rather than darts, place your adjusted fitting pattern under your fashion pattern to serve as a guide, adding darts where necessary.

For some garment styles—like princess seaming—divide the amount of change needed between the front and the side fronts. Follow the illustrations in making your alterations. You should always test the alterations in muslin **before** cutting into your fashion fabric.

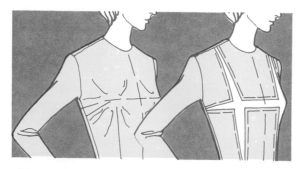
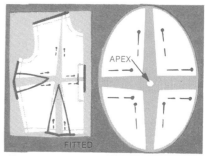

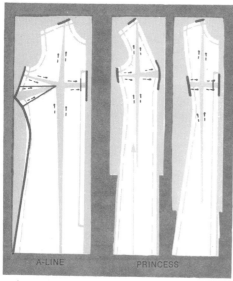
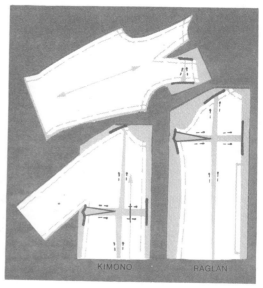

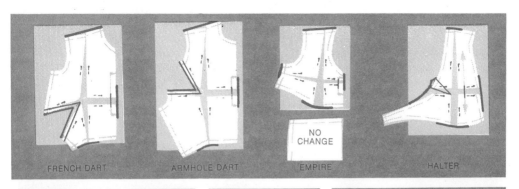

FRENCH DART   ARMHOLE DART   EMPIRE   HALTER

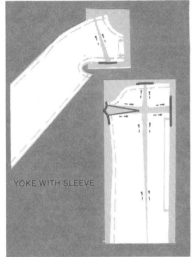

YOKE WITH SLEEVE

YOKED

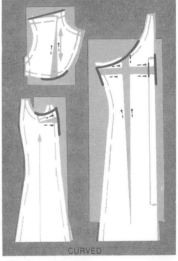

CURVED

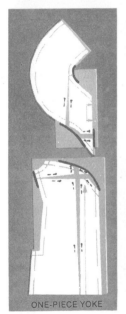

ONE-PIECE YOKE

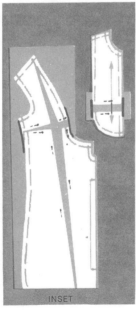

INSET

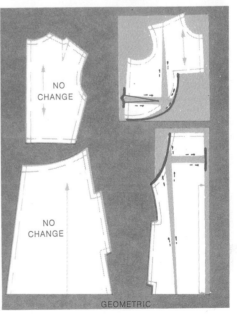

GEOMETRIC

HIGH BUST: Your bustline may be too high, in which case you must change the bustline on your fitting muslin and pattern. The bust darts will fall too far beneath the bust, and the garment bust shaping will be located beneath your own. Use measurement 14 on pages 22–23 to find your bust point.

Draw a line across the muslin where the bust point should be placed. Open the side seam, release the dart, and re-stitch in the new position along your marking; end the darts according to the location of the apex of your bust (see Dart Length, pages 159–160). Raise front darts as shown. Re-stitch the side seam and try on the muslin to check the correction. *This alteration should be applied to all styles with underarm darts,* no matter what their angle.

To alter styles that have bust shaping without darts, such as the princess style, place your adjusted fitting pattern under the dartless bodice pieces; this will indicate the bust position. Make a fold half the amount needed to be raised above the armhole notch. Slash the pattern below the bust shaping and spread the pattern the same amount. Re-draw the shoulder, front, and armhole cutting lines to bring the bodice back to its original shape. To alter the bustline of other special designs, see the illustrations below. Always test styles without darts in muslin *before* you begin to cut into your fashion fabric.

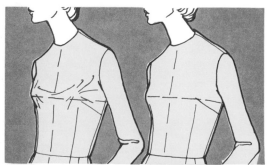

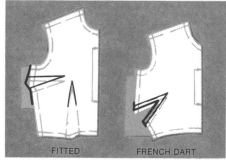

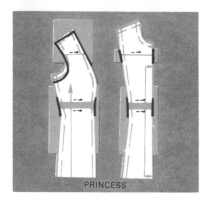

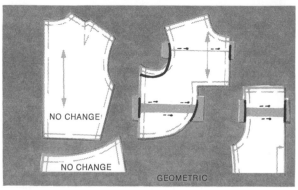

LOW BUST: You may find that your bustline is too low for the bust cupping of the muslin, and the fit is distorted. Use measurement 14 on pages 22–23 to find your bust point. Draw a line across your muslin where the bust point should be. Release the side seams and the darts. Re-stitch darts in the proper position, following the marked line and ending the darts in relation to the apex of your bust. (See Dart Length at bottom of page). Lower front darts in the same manner. Re-stitch the side seams, and try on the muslin to check the corrected fit. *This alteration should be applied to all underarm bust darts, regardless of their angle or the garment style.* Correct dart position on bodice front.

To alter styles which have bust shaping but no darts—like a princess style—place your altered fitting pattern under the dartless pattern pieces to serve as a guide. Slash through pattern at armhole notch and spread the amount needed to lower the bustline. Below bustline, make a fold half the amount bustline was lowered to preserve the bodice length. Raise the armhole below the armhole notch and re-draw all other interrupted cutting lines as indicated. To alter the bustline of other designs with special seaming, see the illustration below. Test styles without darts in muslin *before* cutting fashion fabric.

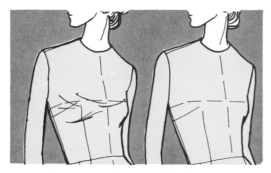
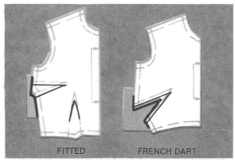
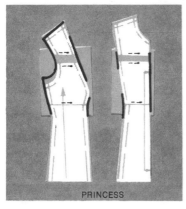
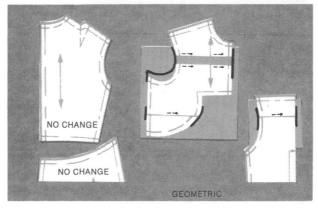

DART LENGTH: If the bust darts on your fitting shell do not fit your contours, you can alter your bodice by re-shaping the darts since the position of the bust apex varies with each woman. The underarm darts should end ½" from the apex, and the front darts ½"-1" below the apex. Lengthening or shortening darts may not be enough to give a proper fit. Refer to the preceding alterations for high and low bustlines for further instruction.

Styles with bust darts at the armhole or shoulder seam can be lengthened or shortened as indicated on page 160. *Always test in muslin before cutting into your fashion fabric.* For French darts, do not cut out the "V" shape when testing. Fit them and then after stitching, trim to within ⅝" of the dart seam and press open.

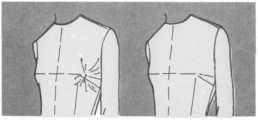

To shorten underarm dart, place a pin on the muslin where dart should end. Release side seam and dart; re-stitch dart to correct length. Re-stitch the side seam and try on to check muslin. Reposition bodice front dart the same way. Transfer changes to pattern.

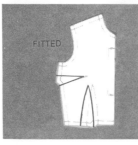
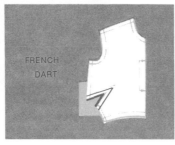
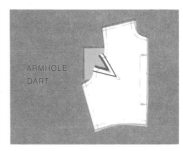

To lengthen underarm dart, place a pin on the muslin where the dart should end. Release the side seam and dart, and shape underarm dart to your bust contour. Re-

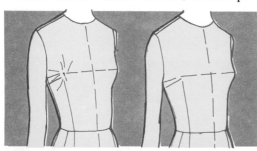

stitch the dart to the correct length. Restitch the side seam and try on the muslin to check the correction that you have made. For the bodice front dart, correct the position in the same way. Transfer changes to your pattern piece as indicated. Always test style variations in muslin before you begin cutting into your fashion fabric.

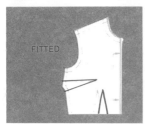
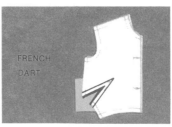
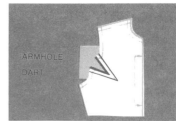

Chest

Your bone structure is the major cause of alterations in the chest—the rib cage and the collar bone control the length of the bodice. Poor posture or figure flaws may necessitate alterations in the armhole area or between shoulder and bust. These chest alterations affect the front of your garment and should be transferred to related pattern pieces only. Back pattern pieces will not be affected.

HOLLOW CHEST: The bodice wrinkles and gaps between bust and neckline due to excess fabric. To correct, pin out wrinkles, tapering to armhole or shoulder seams. Transfer the alteration to bodice front pattern piece. Test altered raglan, kimono, and princess styles in muslin before cutting fashion fabric.

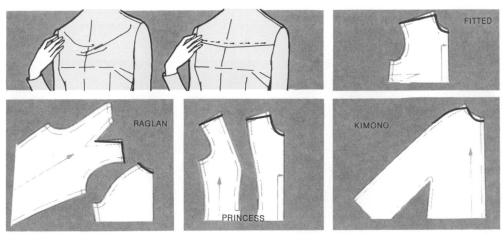

NARROW UPPER CHEST: Excess fabric appears around the armhole above the bust. This problem may be found in combination with a high, rounded back.

To correct muslin, remove the sleeve and open shoulder seam to the neck seamline. Pin a dart deep enough to remove the wrinkles. The back shoulder seam should be eased to fit the shortened front shoulder seam. Transfer alteration to front bodice pattern piece by slashing through armhole and up through center of shoulder area. Then lap edges to decrease chest area. For raglan, kimono, and princess styles, take out excess fabric at seam as indicated. *Test* the alteration first in muslin.

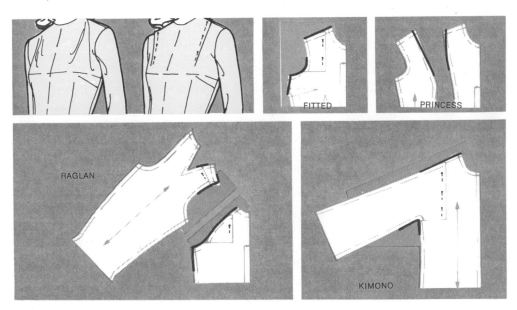

PIGEON CHEST: When the collar and breast bones protrude, the bodice pulls above the bust and distorts the armhole seam. To correct, release armhole seam; slash across the front above the bust and up through the center of shoulder area to the seam. Insert strips of fabric under slash and spread as necessary to accommodate body contour. Keep slashed edges flat and baste securely to fabric strip. Transfer alteration to front pattern pieces as indicated. *Test* style variations in muslin.

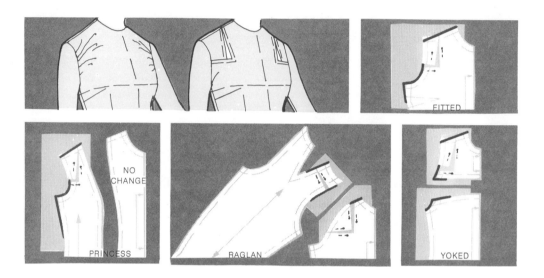

Back

After the shoulders, sleeves, and front section of your garment have been fitted to your contours, you can focus on the back. Virtually all alterations made on the back portion of your garment will affect only that area of your muslin unless the style includes raglan or kimono sleeves. In most cases, back alterations are needed to correct fitting problems caused by bone structure and/or posture. If your fitting shell does not mold smoothly over your body contours from the neck to the hem edge, one or more of the following alterations may be all that is needed to correct the fit By adjusting your pattern to your circumference measurements before constructing the muslin, you have allowed the proper girth for your torso. If bone structure and posture cause further wrinkling, pulling, and uneven draping, alterations will be necessary to achieve a garment which hangs smoothly.

VERY ERECT BACK: This is apparent when excess fabric in the bodice back creates parallel wrinkles across the back above shoulder blades. Corrections can accommodate your erect posture. Pin out the wrinkles, tapering to the armhole or shoulder seams at location of problem. Alter bodice back pattern piece by shortening the center back length; re-draw neck and shoulder edges.

Make the same alteration on raglan, kimono, and princess styles on appropriate pattern pieces. Test in muslin *before* cutting into your fashion fabric.

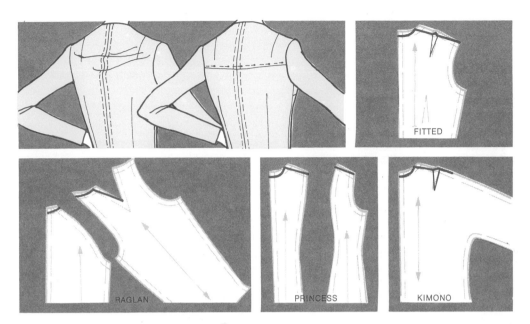

HOLLOW SHOULDER BLADE: Excess fabric will cause vertical wrinkles between the shoulder seam and the fullest part of the shoulder blade. Your bone structure has created a hollow in this area. Release shoulder seam. Pin a dart in back deep enough to eliminate wrinkles. Then ease the front shoulder seam to fit. Transfer alterations to back bodice pattern pieces as indicated.

Make same alteration on the back pattern pieces of raglan, kimono, and princess styles. Test in muslin *before* cutting your fashion fabric.

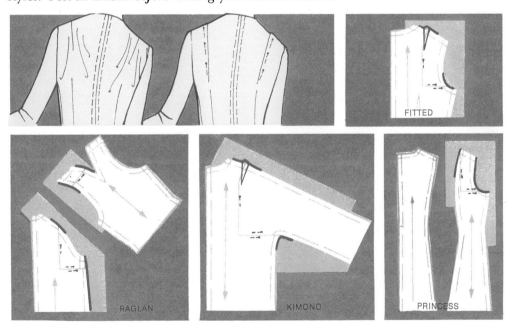

HIGH, ROUNDED BACK (DOWAGER'S HUMP): Frequently a problem of mature women, this need not be a fitting difficulty. It is a figure flaw which may be caused by extremely rounded shoulders, too. The bodice wrinkles and pulls across the shoulders and in the areas adjacent to the sleeve caps; the back length is too short. This will cause the hemline to be uneven in a jacket, or the bodice to pull at the waist seam.

To alter your fitting muslin, slash perpendicular to the grainline across the muslin between the armhole seams. Release the stitching from the zipper between the slash and the neck edge. Insert strips of fabric under the slashed edges, and spread the muslin the amount needed to fit properly and comfortably. Baste the strips of fabric to each half of the bodice back so there is an opening; keep the slashed edges flat. Fill in the muslin at the back neck edge with other fabric strips to extend the edges to the opening. Add darts to the neck edge to fit the curve of the body.

To transfer the alteration to the pattern, slash pattern horizontally as indicated, and again from the neck edge to the first slash. Increase the center back length the amount needed, keeping center back seamlines aligned. Connect cutting lines and re-draw shoulder dart if needed. Add a neckline dart, as indicated.

FITTED
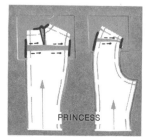
PRINCESS

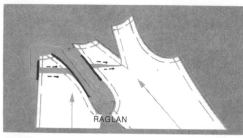
RAGLAN
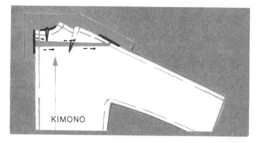
KIMONO

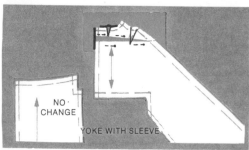
NO CHANGE
YOKE WITH SLEEVE
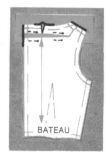
BATEAU
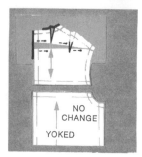
NO CHANGE
YOKED

NARROW BACK: Even though the bodice front has been fitted perfectly, a narrow back will cause the back of the fitting muslin to be too full in the shoulder area and too loose above the waistline seam. An A-line fitting garment may be longer at the back than at the front hemline and may hang away from the body at the shoulders and waist. To fit the garment properly, the back must be taken in to drape smoothly over the body contours.

To alter the back, pin out the excess fabric by uniting each shoulder and waistline dart in a continuous dart from shoulder to waist. To transfer the change to the fitted or A-line back pattern piece, connect the darts.

For a princess style, reduce by taking deeper side back seams.

For garments which have no back darts, slash pattern to shoulder seamline to eliminate excess girth. Clip seam allowance so pattern will lie flat (not shown). Lowered necklines and princess styles are altered as indicated. Test in muslin *before* cutting into your fashion fabric.

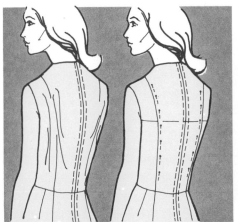
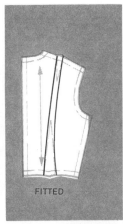

FITTED

SCOOP

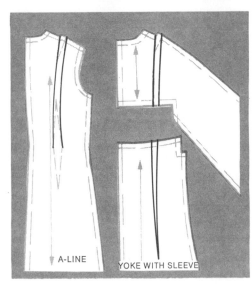

A-LINE

YOKE WITH SLEEVE

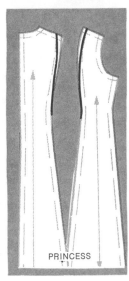

PRINCESS

YOKED

LARGE BACK OR PROMINENT SHOULDER BLADES: An oft-encountered figure variation, a large back or prominent shoulder blades will cause the garment to pull and wrinkle across the widest area of the back. The fabric binds, and the absence of wearing ease makes it difficult to raise your arms. The strain at the armhole seam could be enough to break the threads unless the back is altered.

To correct, release the stitching at the shoulder seams, shoulder darts, and side seams. At the most curved area, slash across the back of your muslin perpendicular to the lengthwise grain. Then slash up to the point of the dart, parallel to the grain. Continue the slash through the center of the dart. Insert strips of fabric under the slashed edges and spread the amount needed; baste the strips in place. Shape the dart to fit the body contour; re-stitch the seam. Try on muslin and test: raise your arms to check fit and wearing ease. To transfer the alteration to the back pattern piece, re-draw the dart. For other styles, alter back pattern pieces as indicated, adding shoulder darts if none exist. Always test in muslin *before* cutting fashion fabric so you can shape darts to fit the shoulder contour exactly.

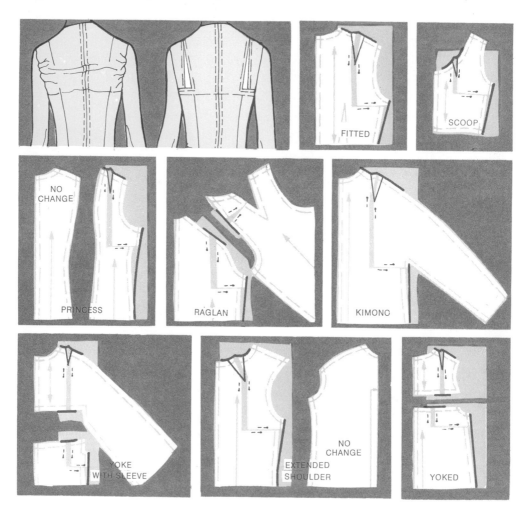

SWAY BACK: Caused by body contour or posture, a sway back can mar the lines of your garment unless altered to fit. A smooth, even line will be interrupted by wrinkles across the back below the waistline in a figure having a sway back. To alter the muslin, pin out the excess fabric, tapering the fold to the side seams. On the fitting pattern, shorten the center back the same amount. Re-draw the cutting line, and re-draw and shorten darts as shown. Shorten the center back of the A-line and princess styles as indicated. Because the skirt portion will be shifted off grain by this correction, you must re-draw the grainline. Also, re-draw the lower part of the dart, shortening it to fit your contours.

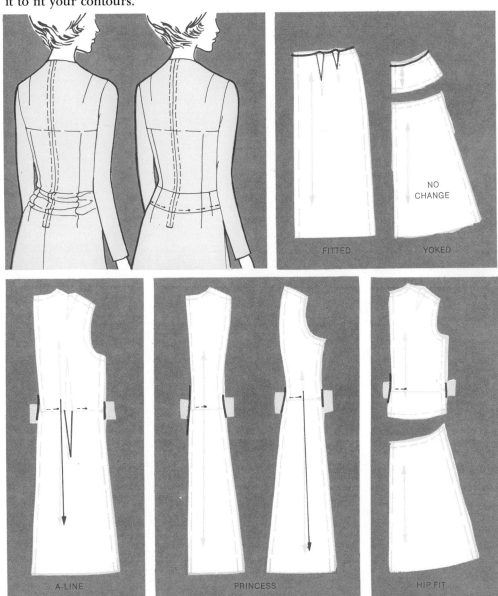

FLAT BUTTOCKS: The muslin shell hangs in loose wrinkles and collapses over a flat buttocks. Because the garment allows for fullness not present, the hem will hang lower in the back than in the front. To fit, release the stitching in the waist and back darts. Re-pin the darts to the shape of the body. To even the hemline, pin out excess fabric the length of the skirt and across the hipline as shown. To transfer the alteration to the back pattern piece, re-draw darts, then pin a tuck the amount needed parallel to the grainline. Shorten the center back length the same amount that was decreased horizontally. On an A-line garment, remove the stitching from the zipper below the back bustline markings. Release the back darts and re-pin them to fit; they can be shorter and narrower. To preserve the waist circumference, reduce it at the center back and side seams.

For a princess style, reduce at the side, side back, and center back seam to fit. For yoke-seamed skirts, alter as indicated. Always be sure to test in muslin *before* cutting into your fashion fabric.

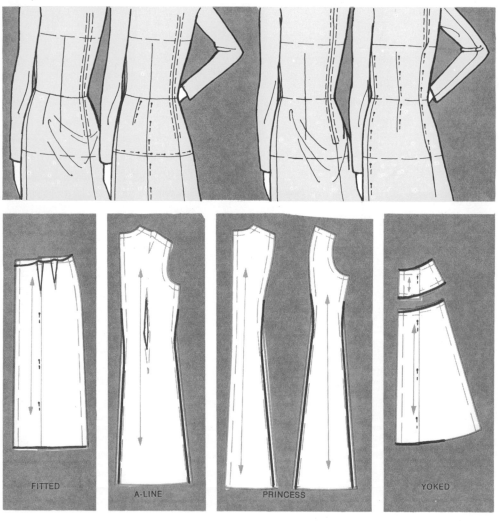

FITTED

A-LINE

PRINCESS

YOKED

LARGE BUTTOCKS OR LARGE BACK AT TOP OF HIPS: Excess flesh due to lack of exercise or being overweight creates wrinkles between the waistline and hipline; the fabric is pulled and the side seams are strained. The garment is shorter at the back hemline than at the front. To correct a fitted garment with a waist seam, release the skirt darts and the waist seam. Re-pin darts to fit smoothly, shortening and widening them. Add to the side seams the amount reduced from the waist circumference by widening the darts. Add to the center back length to even the hemline, if necessary. Alter the pattern as illustrated.

For an A-line style, remove the stitching from the zipper below the back bustline marking, back darts, side seams, and center back seam. Add strips of fabric, spread the amount needed, and baste. Re-pin the darts to fit. Transfer the alteration to the pattern, as shown.

For a princess style and yoked-seam skirts, alter back pattern pieces as indicated. Test in muslin *before* cutting into your fashion fabric.

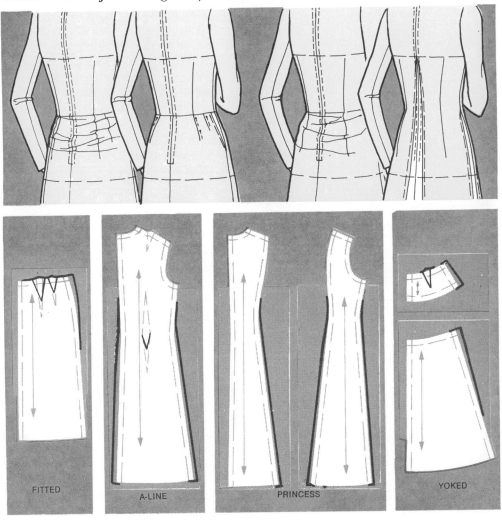

FITTED A-LINE PRINCESS YOKED

Hips

By making the circumference adjustments explained in Book II, your muslin fitting shell will have adequate girth in the hip area. However, there remain several figure variations around the hips which may require more extensive fitting than can be provided by circumference adjustments alone. Bone structure, posture, and excess flesh affect hip fit. To be flattering, a garment should drape smoothly and evenly across the hip, buttock, and upper thigh areas. Be particularly alert to your fitting needs throughout the hip area in a fitted garment design.

You will find that the hip area is comparatively easy to fit, so do not hesitate to experiment with your muslin to achieve perfect and personalized fit.

PROTRUDING HIP BONES: Any garment designed to closely fit body contours will reveal protruding hip bones. The front pulls between the hip bones and the bone structure is visually emphasized rather than blended into the figure.

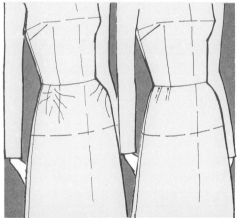

To correct the fit, release the stitching from the front darts and waist seam. Reposition the darts to make the muslin fit smoothly over the hip bones; re-shape darts as needed. Transfer alteration to the front pattern piece. If this has reduced the waistline circumference, add this amount to the side seams.

The alteration is not usually needed in A-line styles. To alter a fitted princess style, adapt the side and side front seams to fit; add darts if necessary. Alter skirts with fitted yokes as indicated. Test in muslin *before* cutting your fashion fabric.

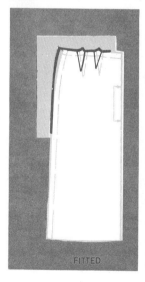

FITTED

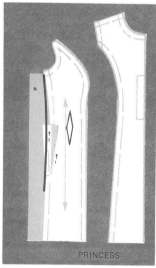

PRINCESS

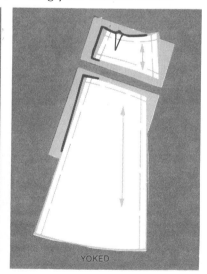

YOKED

170

ONE LARGE HIP: While all figures are slightly asymmetrical, a special alteration for this is needed only when the garment appears to be distorted. One large hip will exaggerate the fit and cause an uneven hemline. Also, the skirt will pull up on both the front and back sides of the large hip. In some styles, this may not be evident, but in a fitted garment it is of great significance.

To alter a fitting muslin with a waist seam, release the darts, and the waist and side seams where the large hip protrudes. Lower the skirt until the grainlines and hem are straight. Insert strips of fabric at sides and waist; baste. Re-pin darts to fit. For an A-line garment, release the side seam and back dart on the shorter side. Insert fabric strips, spread the amount needed, and baste in place. Pin the back dart to fit the shape of the body.

To transfer this alteration to your pattern pieces, you must make an exact tracing of the front and back pattern pieces—you will then enlarge half the pattern and leave the other half unchanged. Transfer alteration to the side needed (illustrations show the *right* hip altered).

For princess styles, adapt the method used for A-line styles to alter pattern pieces; then test in muslin *before* cutting into your fashion fabric.

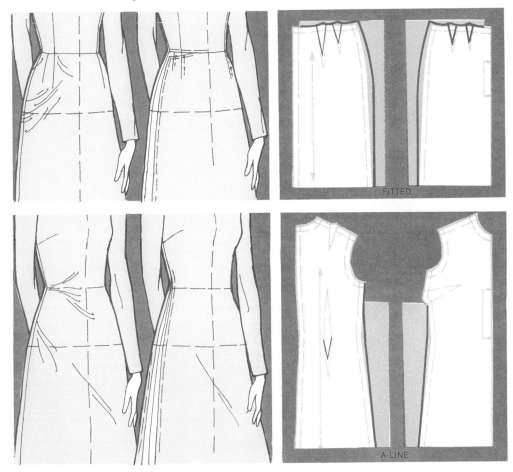

FITTED

A-LINE

THIGH BULGE: No matter how small or large a woman's figure, fit may be distorted by thigh bulge. On a fitted garment, the skirt pulls and wrinkles at upper thigh just below hipline. It may not be noticeable in loosely fitted styles. Hip circumference is not affected by heavy thighs in this problem. Locating the thigh bulge is explained on pages 22–23.

To correct a fitted muslin, release the side seam to the hipline. Add strips of fabric to the muslin, spread to fit, and baste strips in place. Transfer ¼ of the amount needed for the alteration to the front pattern piece; slash at the same point on the side seam, then down to the hem, paralleling the grainline. Re-draw new cutting lines. Alter the back pattern piece the same amount.

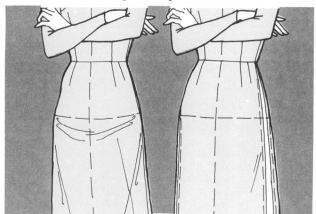
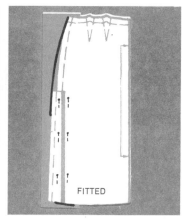

Abdomen

Adjusting the circumference of your pattern has provided you with the necessary girth in the abdomen area, but alterations may be required to accommodate your body contour. Posture or fleshiness due to lack of exercise or overweight can be the basis for alteration. Unsightly wrinkles and pulling must be eliminated.

LARGE ABDOMEN: A large abdomen will affect the hang of your skirt, causing it to ride up in front and the side seams to pull forward. For garments with a waist seam, release front waist seam and darts. Drop skirt front until it hangs evenly. Insert a fabric strip and baste it to the top of the skirt. Re-pin darts to fit your contour. If this alteration makes the waistline smaller, add the necessary amount to the side seams. Re-stitch darts and seams and check the fit again. Transfer alteration to the pattern piece, lengthening the center front as needed and re-drawing darts according to your contours.

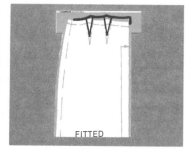

172

An A-line garment is altered by slashing the front up to the bust area. Insert fabric strips and spread edges the amount necessary for side seams, waistline, and hipline to fall into position. Baste fabric strips to slashed edges. Transfer alteration to pattern front, slashing through the bust dart to make the pattern lie flat; allow edges to overlap.

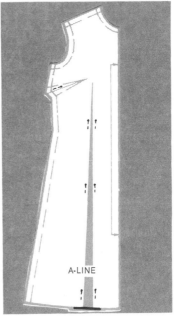

FLAT ABDOMEN: A flat abdomen also affects the hang of the skirt; the hem is uneven due to the wrinkling of excess fabric through this area. The garment allows length not needed by your figure. To correct garments with a waist seam, pin out excess fabric between the waist and hipline until the hem edge is even. Taper the fold at the side seams. Transfer alteration to the front pattern piece, re-shaping darts and decreasing center front length.

For A-line garments, pin out excess fabric in the form of a double-pointed dart which extends from the bust to the hip level.

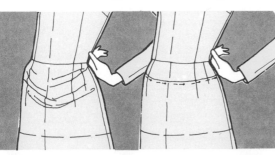

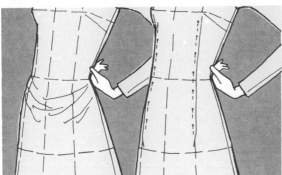

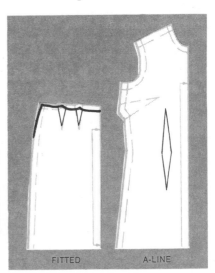

The Pants Look
Made Great

Although they are among the easiest clothes in the world to make and wear, pants demand the most precise fit possible if they are to be super creations. Cut is all-important, because no amount of fitting after the fact can salvage a pair of pants which were not adjusted and altered to coincide with your proportions. Altering a pants basic muslin to your individual contours is crucial. Regardless of the style you have chosen, a basic pants pattern adjusted and then altered to personalize its fit will guarantee that each successive pair of pants you make will be flawlessly in step with your contours. This includes jumpsuits — fitted, semi-fitted, or full; pants skirts of all lengths; pleated, yoked, and hip-hugger pants; and any other style of pants with or without a waistband, and any special leg styling. All pants have one thing in common: they must be adapted to the individual contours of your waist, hip, and crotch.

Altering Pants For You

On the following pages you will find alterations which will remedy problems in fit due to irregularities in posture, bone structure, weight, or distribution of flesh. Expect these problems to be highlighted when you put on your pants fitting muslin for the first time. The waist and hip fit required for pants will tell quite a bit about you — from the tiniest thigh bulge to an ample derrière.

Even though the length and circumference adjustments were made before you cut out your muslin fitting shell, alterations may be needed to exactly fit your body contours. Length adjustments are easily made to satisfy your needs, but circumference adjustments cannot allow for asymmetrical figure variations. When fitting pants, many women expect more than it can ever do from a simple crotch length adjustment; this is designed merely to bring the crotch curve of the pants into position so it follows your body without wrinkling or binding. The crotch length adjustment does not compensate for heavy thighs, a large abdomen, or flat buttocks — these are figure flaws requiring alterations and must be worked out in a muslin fitting shell.

Jumpsuits are a pants variation made for our lifestyles today. Jumpsuits with a *waist seam,* whether it falls at the waist, or is raised or lowered, are handled just as you would the bodice of your basic fitting shell and your basic fitting pants muslin; the waist seam of each becomes the common denominator. However, jumpsuits with a *cut-in-one bodice and pants* require more detailed alterations (similar to the ones needed for A-line styles); you cannot simply raise or lower the waist seamline and shift darts to compensate for figure flaws. Making a muslin will help in achieving satisfactory fit in this type of jumpsuit.

In analyzing your pants fitting shell (pages 132–133), you may find that you need to make only minor changes for perfect fit. If so, we suggest that you use the fitting techniques for pants found in Book I, pages 69–71. These will guide you in molding your fashion fabric to perfection.

For those who find that they will require pants alterations, the procedure used to adapt the pattern is explained on pages 100–101. Since most figure flaws are localized, often only one pattern piece will be changed. In others, the change may be the same for both front and back; only the front pattern piece will be shown. The changes for cutting lines and darts will be indicated with *bold lines;* alter the pattern to your needs as indicated by the illustrations.

The most important aspect of altering your pants muslin is to understand fitting the garment to your individual body contours. As you gain knowledge of fitting, you will find that the adaptation of all pants patterns and designs to your contours is easy and will ensure a perfect fit every time.

LARGE ABDOMEN: A large abdomen distorts the whole front of your pants— from the crotch level to the waist—because not enough fabric has been allowed to accommodate your contour. Pulling at the crotch and inseam as well as the crosswise wrinkles appearing below the waist can be eliminated in a fitting muslin, but not in fashion fabric after your pants have been cut. Release waist, inseam, and darts, and drop the top of the pants until the side seams fall into position. Add a strip of fabric to the top of the pants and to the front inner leg seam; baste securely in place. Pin the darts to fit the contour of your body. Transfer the alteration to your front pattern piece.

For styles with front pleats or pants with an elasticized waist, alter according to preceding instructions. Jumpsuits whose bodice and pants are cut-in-one will require slashing across the waist to the middle of each front section, and then diagonally to the knee to get the extra length needed. Test these styles in muslin *before* cutting into your fashion fabric.

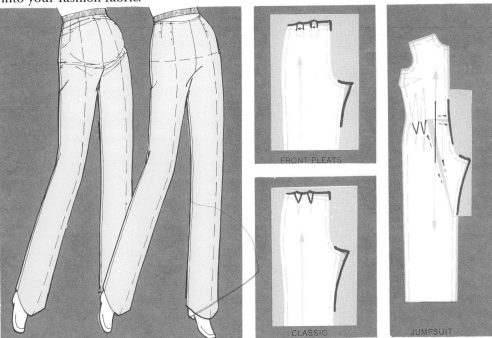

FRONT PLEATS

CLASSIC

JUMPSUIT

PROTRUDING HIP BONES: This figure flaw is attributed to bone structure, and creates pulling and wrinkling over the high hip area. To correct, release darts and re-pin them to fit your contour. Depending on your bone structure, shorten or widen the darts as necessary. If this makes the waistline smaller, add the required amount to side seams. Transfer the alteration to front pattern piece.

For pants with a pleated front, alter according to the preceding instructions. This alteration is not usually necessary for pants with elasticized waists. To alter jumpsuits with the bodice and pants cut-in-one, slash to the center of the pattern and then diagonally to the knee to give you extra width to fit darts. Test style variations in muslin *before* cutting into your fashion fabric.

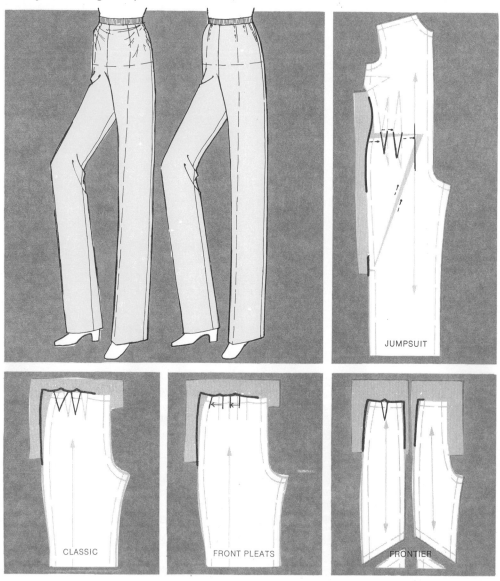

JUMPSUIT

CLASSIC

FRONT PLEATS

FRONTIER

THIGH BULGE: Many women have this problem regardless of their bone structure, weight, or posture. It appears below the full hipline, and seems to be the widest point of the body even though circumference measurements of the hip might not agree. Crosswise wrinkles occur across the front and back of the pants due to the strain at the side seams and inseams. Release the stitching at the side seams, and spread the amount needed until all wrinkles disappear and the pants legs hang smoothly. Insert strips of fabric under the edges and baste securely.

When transferring alteration to pattern pieces, divide the amount equally between the front and back pattern pieces; at the widest point of the thigh bulge, slash the pattern from the side seam approximately 3″ into the garment. Slash from the innermost point to the knee. Any style of pants, as well as jumpsuits with bodice and pants cut-in-one, can be altered this way. Test style variations in muslin *before* cutting into your fashion fabric.

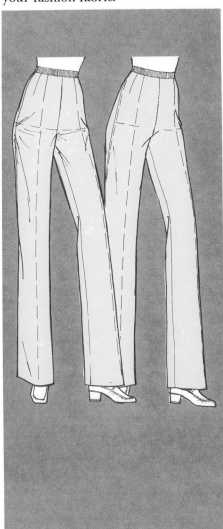
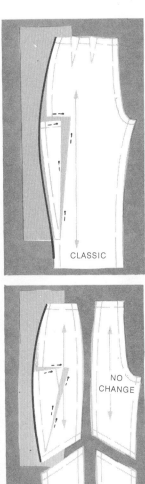
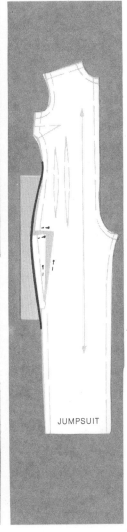

CLASSIC

NO CHANGE

NO CHANGE

FRONTIER

JUMPSUIT

SWAY BACK: Through posture, bone structure, or excess weight, many women have a sway back. It is as apparent in pants as in a skirt—the same wrinkling occurs in both below the waistline at the back. To correct your muslin pants shell, pin out the excess fabric, tapering the fold to the side seams. Release and re-pin the darts, reducing their length. To transfer the alteration to the pattern, decrease the length at the center back.

Make the same alterations on pants with an elasticized waist and re-draw the casing foldline. For pants with a back yoke, reduce the yoke pattern piece at center back. To alter a jumpsuit whose bodice and pants are cut-in-one, slash at the waist and lap the amount needed to shorten center back length. Test the pants style variations in muslin *before* cutting into your fashion fabric.

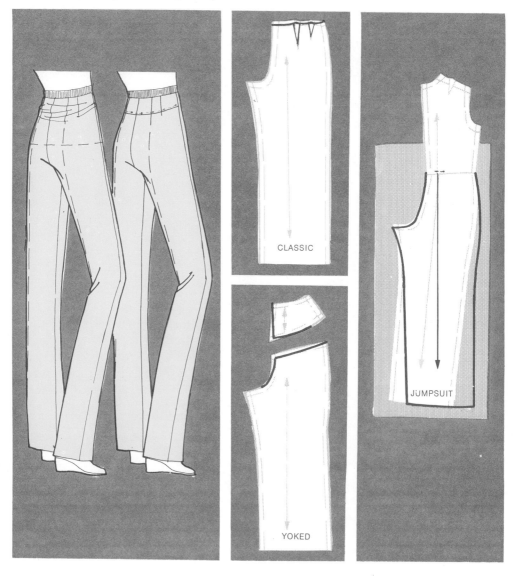

CLASSIC

YOKED

JUMPSUIT

FLAT BUTTOCKS: Wrinkles form at the buttocks area, and the pants sag because the body lacks the contour to support the fullness. To alter, pin out the excess along the high hipline and down each leg. Taper folds to nothing at the side seams, waist, and knee. Release waist darts and re-pin them to fit the body curves; work out the extra waist circumference at the side seams. Transfer the alteration to the pattern. For another method, see Seam Fitting, page 181.

Pants which feature an elastic encased waist and pants having a back yoke are altered in the same way. For jumpsuits with bodice and pants cut-in-one, slash at the waist and lap the amount needed to reduce the back length. Starting at the first slash, fold out excess girth, tapering to knee. Test in muslin *before* cutting into your fashion fabric.

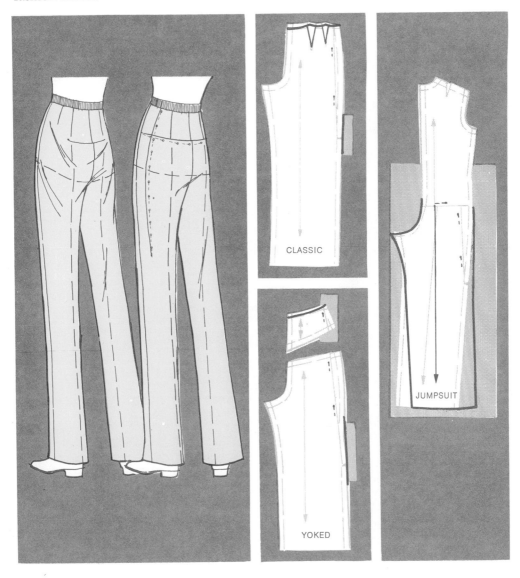

CLASSIC

YOKED

JUMPSUIT

LARGE BUTTOCKS: While the hip circumference of your pants will have been accommodated by purchasing your pattern by hip size, large buttocks may require more fabric for the pants to fit properly and comfortably; also, the contours of the front of your body may take away needed girth. The muslin pants shell pulls down across the back, and the side seams and the inseams are wrinkled and strained through the hip area. To correct, remove the stitching from the darts. Also release the inseams to the knee. Lower the top of the pants into position and add strips of fabric to the top so the pants reach the waist; also add to the back inseams until the pants drape smoothly. Pin darts to fit the shape of the body, and increase the waist at the side seams if needed. Transfer the alteration to the pattern as shown.

Make the same alteration for pants having an elasticized waist and re-draw the casing foldline. Alter pants with a back yoke as shown. For jumpsuits which have bodice and pants that are cut-in-one, slash at the waist and then diagonally to the knee to get the extra length that is needed. Be sure to test the alteration in muslin *before* cutting into your fashion fabric.

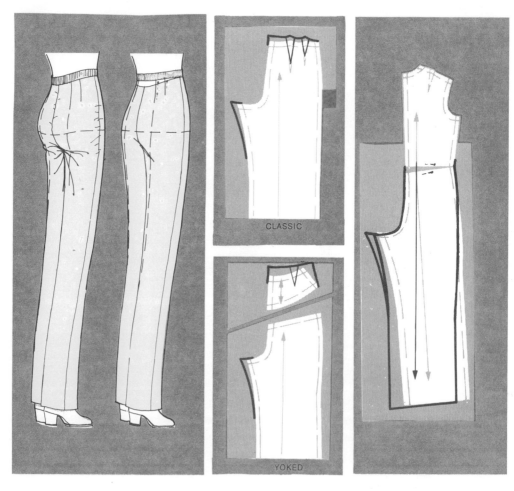

CLASSIC

YOKED

SEAM FITTING: A more stylized way to alter pants is to contour the backs of the legs with seam fitting, or to taper the legs at each side seam and inseam.

Contouring the backs of the legs is a combined fitting technique and styling feature. You can use it to create closely fitted pants. On each leg of your muslin, pin out the excess fabric from the back dart closest to the center to the hem; try to keep the seam parallel to the grainline and in a straight line down the center back of each leg. Re-shape the darts to your particular needs. Make an effort to preserve the style lines of your pants, even though the seam will vary in depth as it follows the shape of your body.

Transfer the new seamlines to your pattern. Remember that pants with flaring legs are not always on the straight grain below the knee; for these, keep the lower part of the new seam at the center of the leg.

Tapering is another technique for customizing pants. First, note the knee marking on your muslin. For snugly fitted pants legs, decrease at the side and inseams. Do not fit the knee area too tightly, as the pants would wear out more quickly. Divide the amount to be reduced between the two seams, tapering to the crotch and hip. Make sure to leave ample circumference at knee and instep.

To alter the pattern, mark ¼ of the intended amount to be decreased at the hemline of each seam. Evenly draw new cutting lines from the hem up to the knee, then taper to the crotch and along the side seam. Taper pants with flaring legs gradually from the hemline to the knee; then taper both seams as above.

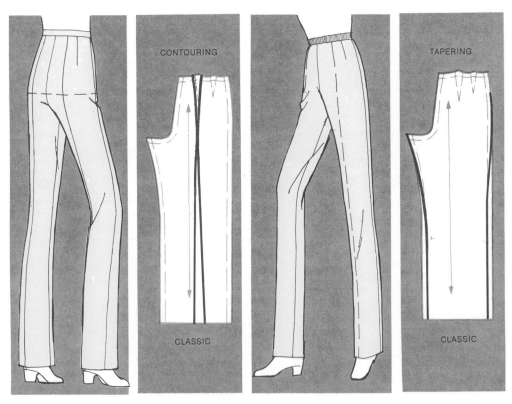

Perfect Fit
Made Memorable

The greatest value of the adjustments and alterations you have made lies in their being repeatedly used to build fit into each fashion project you attempt. It is quite possible that once they have been discovered, the variations between your figure and the standard will remain relatively constant. Barring any changes in your body due to weight loss or gain or to re-proportioning, a permanent record of your figure and its fitting requirements—in effect, a master pattern—will be a priceless sewing tool to possess and use again and again.

Having arrived at this point in the creation of perfectly fitted clothes, it only remains for you to refine fit in terms of each fashion design and fabric you choose. The adjustments and alterations which you have found to be necessary are your general rules of thumb in establishing fit. These must be followed by the fitting specifics detailed in Book I which are responsible for molding fashion fabrics of many characters to your figure. The reaction of an individual fabric to a design and your figure cannot be accounted for in adjustments and alterations. Your ultimate success in creating clothes which fit perfectly depends on combining pattern adjustments and alterations with the interpretation of fit in any fashion fabric you might select. After cutting out your fashion garment, turn to Book I and focus on your particular fitting needs and goals.

Fitting Tools

You have made the necessary pattern adjustments, constructed "Vogue's Guide to Perfect Fit of Fitted Garments" in muslin, and made a pants fitting shell in muslin. Having altered these to fit your individual contours, you must then transfer both adjustments and alterations directly to your basic pattern pieces. The result is a pattern which has personalized fit and which can be used in adapting other styles to your individual frame and contours. Your original tissue pattern pieces may, after being adjusted and altered, need some support to function effectively as a master pattern throughout your many sewing ventures.

Other valuable assets are your muslin fitting shells. It is advisable to try them on periodically to check their fit. If your weight or contours change regularly, use your muslin as a gauge, and make further alterations in it to keep your master patterns up to date with these fluctuations. On the following pages, you will find information pertinent to the use of your two most valuable sewing tools—the altered muslins and your master patterns of fully adapted flat pattern pieces for dresses and for pants. The use of these will facilitate and professionalize the fitting and construction of every garment you choose to make, and you will have assurance of achieving superb results before you begin.

Fitted Dress and Pants Muslins

Little is more satisfying than knowing that the garment you are beginning will, when finished, fit you beautifully. The time and effort spent in creating a perfectly fitting basic dress and pants in muslin will prove invaluable in making other designs. Your muslin and master pattern will save time and ensure perfect fit. Regard them as primary tools in creating a perfectly fitting garment.

Consider your altered *muslin* a fitting check—it should be tried on before you adapt any fashion pattern to your master pattern. Check to see whether a loss or gain of weight affects the fit of your basic muslin shell, requiring that further alterations of the garment be made. Even if your weight remains constant, your contours may change from those to which you altered your muslin. When you try on your fitting shell, you will immediately see changes to be made and can correct them before adapting your fashion pattern. Your muslin is invaluable in this respect and should not be disassembled. Make your master pattern a durable fitting tool according to the instructions given on pages 184–185.

Store your muslin fitting garment in a closet on a padded hanger. Hang your pants muslin by clipping the hemlines to a special pants hanger or by folding them over the crossbar of a padded hanger; fold the pants legs so that side seams and inseams are aligned. If necessary, press your muslin before trying it on.

Making Your Master Pattern

Preserving your basic fitting patterns is one of the most important steps you can take. Using these will ensure that every garment you sew has within it the potential to be a fitting masterpiece.

A PERMANENT RECORD: To make your master pattern work for you, mark the exact amount of change needed on the pattern—use one color pen for length adjustments, a second color for circumference adjustments, and a third for alterations. Mark the exact amount of any change; i.e. $3/4'' \rightarrow$ for circumference, $1/2''$ ↑ for length. Use a plus (+) to denote the amount you lengthened or enlarged the pattern, and a minus (−) to denote the amount you shortened or reduced the pattern. We must assume that every change you made to make the pattern correspond with your needs was made accurately, and that you maintained the flatness of your pattern by clipping or pleating the seam and/or hem allowances so they would lie flat.

When you have clearly transferred every change, you are ready to make it a permanent record of your needs. There are two ways to do this: you can attach each pattern piece to an iron-on non-woven interfacing, or you can trace the pattern pieces onto a transparent non-woven nylon fabric that is made especially for pattern tracings. When your pattern has been supported or traced, roll it printed side out, around a large cardboard cylinder so the pattern will curl the right way when unrolled. Do not crease or fold the pattern, because you should avoid subjecting it to unnecessary wear and tear.

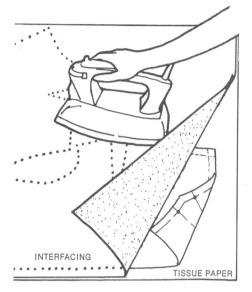

INTERFACING

TISSUE PAPER

Stabilize the Pattern: To make your master pattern durable and to keep your original adjustments and alterations visible, use an iron-on non-woven interfacing as a stiffener. Press the pattern pieces to remove wrinkles and to make sure they are flat.

To attach the interfacing to the pattern pieces, use steam or a hot dry iron, and work on a large padded surface. Place each pattern piece *printed side down* on tissue paper and have the adhesive side of the interfacing on the wrong side of each pattern piece. Use weights to hold the pattern pieces and interfacing in place. Arrange pattern pieces under the interfacing carefully so the fabric is not wasted as grain does not have to be considered. On the right side of the interfacing, press from the center and work toward the edges until the entire surface of the fabric has been fused to each pattern piece. Let the pattern pieces cool, then cut them out. To use your master pattern, turn to page 185 for further information.

Trace the Pattern: It is recommended that you use a ball point or felt-tip pen so the lines will not smudge; it may be helpful to have a thicker pen line for the cutting lines, grainlines, and "Place on Fold" lines, and a finer pen line for the seamlines and darts. Remember to make all lines heavy enough to be easily seen, as you will be placing Vogue fashion patterns on top of your master pattern pieces

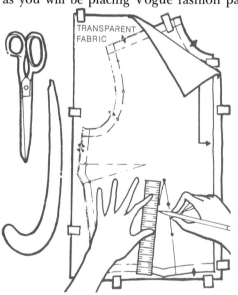

TRANSPARENT FABRIC

in order to evaluate the style ease and wearing ease, as well as the other pertinent information recorded on your master pattern pieces. You will need a large flat surface on which to work. Place a large sheet of white paper under the pattern pieces so the lines will be easier to see. Make sure your pattern is free of wrinkles. Do not use pins to anchor the pattern pieces, as the lines will be distorted; instead use paperweights. As you trace, use your French curve, T-square, yardstick, and see-through ruler to help in duplicating the pattern line for line. When you are ready to use your master pattern, turn to page 185 for further information.

184

Using the Master Pattern: There are many ways your master pattern can be used to help in understanding your fitting needs. On pages 28–30, you will find how to use your master pattern in evaluating wearing ease and style ease in fashion patterns. Here we will show you how to use your master pattern in making the correct adjustments and alterations on your fashion patterns.

For *dresses* that have a raised or lowered waist, pin the bodice and skirt of both the fashion pattern and your master pattern together along the waist seamlines at the centers. Do not try to match the side edges, as doing so will not give you a true picture of where it is best to adapt your fashion pattern to your master pattern. Then slide the master pattern of your dress pattern under the fashion pattern. If your pattern has a sleeve variation—like raglan styling—pin the front sleeve edge to the bodice edge, matching shoulder and underarm indications. You will be able to tell immediately where to make any of your personal adjustments and alterations. Analyze each fashion pattern piece with your master pattern pieces. Make the adjustments and alterations needed so the length and girth will not distort the fashion silhouette.

Your *pants* master pattern will save you a considerable amount of time and headaches when you use it for all pants styles. You will see exactly where to change the fashion pattern so it will agree with your master pattern.

CAUTION: Remember, every fashion pattern is not a fitted pattern like your "Vogue's Guide to Perfect Fit of Fitted Garments." Nor is every pants pattern like the classic style you chose for your pants fitting muslin. Do not use up the style ease instead of making the necessary circumference adjustments or alterations. This would result in a misshapen garment that looks nothing like the fashion illustration on the front of your Vogue Pattern envelope.

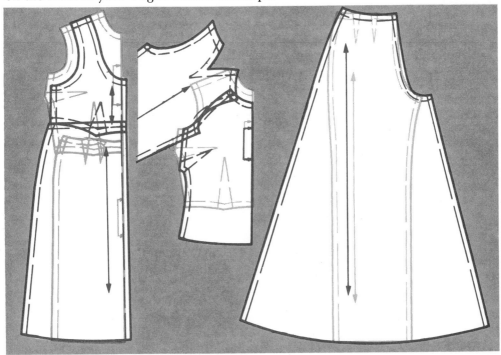

Index